# FROM MODEST BEGINNING TO FINANCIAL FREEDOM

**A Journey Of Endurance, Determination And Courage**

*By*

HERMAN MUKASA

Published By

Bellevue Publishers

www.BellevuePublishers.com

# Contents

# Chapter 1
# INTRODUCTION

"Eriman, akugoba yakuwa ekubo," said my mother, giving me advice on how to deal with problem kids who gave me trouble.

My mother always called me Eriman instead of Herman, my first name. On many occasions, my parents used that Luganda expression, which translates that if someone is chasing you and wanting to catch you, you get hints on how to avoid being apprehended by listening to what the chaser yells out.

You can get hints as to what your best route of escape is and, thus, what your next moves should be. How? By screaming and yelling out loud and alerting other people downhill or uphill that you are running in their direction. Alerting them to be ready to catch you and hold you down. And what do you do once you hear that scream? You change the direction in which you are running. If you were running east, you would change direction and run west, south, or north and away from where you could be apprehended.

Looking back over the years of my life, what my parents used to tell me many years ago has had a lot of meaning as I went through life and achieved what I have been able to achieve. Some of the major decisions that changed my life were because of things I did to prove to people who made negative comments about me; that I was incapable of accomplishing things that were bigger than they could accomplish.

My experiences are commonly encountered by other individuals, especially minorities and people who arrive in the USA from other countries. Being a black person and especially having been born in Africa, society tends to look at us with negative expectations. Quite often, we encounter individuals who discount our achievements and capabilities. The often-talked-about concept of saviorism surfaces many times in our daily lives. Individuals will want to tell us what we should do, even about things they know little about or nothing at all. The fact that I was able to set up investment strategies that ended up being successful was always overlooked. I had people who knew little about my investment strategies but were very willing to give me unsolicited advice on how I should run my investments. Turning down such unsolicited advice occasionally leads to being labeled a crazy person who is going to face a disastrous end.

Shaming of all sorts, but most importantly, negative comments about me for starting life from humble beginnings, was a major driving force in a lot of the decisions I made and achievements I have had through life. The more I was belittled or shamed, the stronger I was driven to do and accomplish things that were far bigger and better than what I would have done or achieved. I reached down into my heart and soul, touched the energy buried deep into me, and utilized that inner energy to do whatever it took to succeed in whatever endeavor I took on. I wanted to prove to those individuals that they were wrong in their thinking. When you set out to shame someone, that person you shame or belittle will go all out to prove to you that by holding your negative beliefs or negative views of them, you are wrong. That becomes a part of their "Why." The reason why they get more driven to achieve their goals.

People tend to spend too much time focusing on how to belittle others when they should focus on improving themselves instead. Their minds are focused on what to do or say to attack the other individual, not thinking of what is needed to advance their well-being. The person engaged in the put-down gets the psychological satisfaction of being more accomplished and needing to do less for their well-being. In this book, I reflect on my life experiences. There were mistakes I made, and there were opportunities that I missed that could have changed my life. I have, however, been able to accomplish many of the aspirations I had in my early life.

My memoir provides a deep insight into the challenges of defying societal prejudices, the sacrifices required to pursue education, and the unwavering determination needed to achieve financial independence. Through these pages, I share not only the milestones of my professional journey but also the failures, fears, and hard-earned lessons that shaped my vision as an investor.

I devote significant time to narrating my journey into investing and wealth-building, outlining various investment strategies that can help achieve financial success. While all investments carry risks, I emphasize the importance of seeking guidance from qualified professionals—such as tax advisors, attorneys, land use experts, and contractors—when making critical decisions. I discuss these strategies from my perspective as an investor, not as an expert in every related field.

By sharing my experiences, I hope this book serves as a beacon of hope and a guide for those navigating the unpredictable path of building something from nothing. For anyone in search of inspiration, I want this memoir to be a reminder that our past does not define our future. No dream is too big, and no beginning is too humble.

Disclaimer: While this book is based on actual events, some names have been changed to respect the privacy of individuals.

# Chapter 2
## My Early Years

I was born and spent the early pre-teen years of my life in Masaka, an area that was one of the original districts of Uganda in the 1960s. It is an area located in southern Uganda and borders Lake Victoria. In those days, the country placed a lot of emphasis on tribal groupings, and much of the governance recognized those groupings, sometimes to the detriment of national unity.

I was born in the Baganda tribal group, which is the largest group in the country by population. The Buganda region is home to one of the ancient African kingdoms that occupied east and central Africa. The five kingdoms were located within present-day Uganda and established circa the thirteenth century. The Buganda kingdom was the largest and strongest of the kingdoms and was ruled by a King or Kabaka.

The kingdom was divided into administrative counties known as masaza, and each county was headed by a county chief who was appointed by the King and thus answerable to the King. Masaka district was included in the county called Buddu and was ruled by a county chief called Sabaddu. My parents told stories of how my great-great-great parents moved to the area having migrated from the eastern part of the Kingdom. According to their stories, my ancestors moved to Masaka sometime in the 1880s, having been sent there to assist in administering the area on behalf of the Kabaka. Several of my ancestors were administrators who oversaw large areas.

The King of Buganda sent trusted individuals as administrators all over the Kingdom, and many of them had close connections or a lineage that connected them to the King.

My parents prided themselves on having a connection to the ancient King of Buganda. At every available opportunity, they wanted us, the younger generation at the time, to be proud of our heritage and the fact that we were connected to the royals of Buganda. At family ceremonies, the boys were always addressed as princes and the girls as princesses. It was a connection that some of my brothers valued greatly. I appreciated the title even though I never went around proclaiming that I had a connection to the royals of Buganda.

This was partly because the King was forced into exile in 1966 when I was young. That followed political turmoil in the country that resulted in all the Uganda kingdoms that existed for centuries being abolished in 1967 and a republic instituted over the entire country. I was too young by then, and by the time I got to the age of understanding what the kingdom meant, it was almost criminal to talk about the King and the Buganda kingdom. I, therefore, was not greatly immersed in the culture and norms of the ancient Kingdom. It was suicidal during those troubled political years under Milton Obote to be associated in any way with the King or identified as the kingdom's previous administrators.

Despite knowing that those risks were always present, my parents regularly educated me on how the Buganda kingdom was ruled. They always hoped that the King would one day return from exile, reclaim his throne, and run the kingdom. I got to understand the kingdom's organization well. Unfortunately, the King died in exile in the United Kingdom. The kingdom was reinstated in 1993, many years after he died in exile in Britain in 1969.

The kingdom's administrative hierarchy of saza or county, gombolola or sub-county, muluka or parish, and village chief enabled the King to effectively control the kingdom. It enabled the king's orders to be implemented throughout the area under his rule. When the European colonialists arrived in the East African region, they found a well-established, effectively administered kingdom. The kingdom's system was so effective that the imperialists left it intact when they colonized Uganda. They gave the Kingdom of Buganda a "Protectorate" status as opposed to other areas of the country, which were put under the direct administration of the colonialists. The colonialists transplanted the administrative system they found in Buganda into other areas of the country and recruited people from the Buganda Kingdom as administrators in those other parts of the country.

The people who lived in those administrative units themselves were grouped into clans. There were 52 clans in total living within those administrative units. Tradition has it that people from the same clan are linked genealogically, to the extent that they refer to themselves as brothers or sisters. They are, therefore, not supposed to intermarry, and such marriages between people of the same clan are considered incest.

My family belongs to the Lion clan, which has a close and significant association with the King and other royals. According to my elders, my great-grandparents were directly and vigorously involved with running the kingdom, performing important duties in the palace. My older brother does not tire of pushing the idea that we all continue to highlight our ties to the monarch, even at this time in our lives. He stresses that it is a cultural thing and a matter of cultural pride.

Having played a role in the administration of the Kingdom, my great-great parents were rewarded with land by the King that covered several square miles in appreciation for their service to the Kingdom. These were lands that were mostly uninhabited at the time. The population in the early 1880s was very sparse. To give you a picture of the conditions at the time, the 1904 census put the population of Uganda at 3.2 million people in a country covering 93,000 square miles. The land that my ancestors got has remained in the family for centuries and has been passed on to descendants as tradition requires.

My father often told us that if we ever inherited the land that the King granted to the family in the 1800s, we should never sell it. The land should always be kept in the family and passed down by inheritance. Those who use it at any time are supposed to pass it on to their heirs once they pass on.

My ancestors saw land as a tool to build wealth by cultivating cash crops to sell, such as coffee and cotton, and to produce food to feed the family. Having land was considered an insurance policy against starvation and one of the essentials to raising a healthy family. Growing up, I knew that if someone failed to feed their family, that would be considered the biggest life failure. That person would be the laughingstock of the community. This belief that my grandparents and then my father instilled in us is one of the foundations that later in my life led me to value real estate as a great avenue to build wealth. That is one of the reasons why I was interested in real estate and got to buy investment properties later in my life.

My parents stressed the importance of getting an education and taught me the need to go to school. They were able to have two of their children graduate from college back in the early 1970s when educational opportunities in the country were limited. They sacrificed a lot for their children because they had come to recognize how vital education was in one's life success. That foundation of valuing education that was instilled in me in my youth is what I, and my other siblings, stand on today. Because of that foundation, we have been able to educate our children, who are now contributing to the world through their jobs and scientific research. Without the sacrifices that our parents made and the seeds they sowed, my siblings and our children most likely would be living different lives without the marketable skills that have helped our families move into the upper and middle-class income levels.

## My Early Schooling

I was born in a family of five girls and six boys. To any standard, that is a large family. When I was five years old, the older brother I followed by birth passed away. He was the one brother I was closest to in age, with an age difference of two years. We used to play all day, and when I started formal schooling, we always walked together to and from school. When he died, I was so sad and felt very lonely. I was so lonely, and on the day following his burial, I sat alone in the house. One of the relatives came to me and tried to cheer me up. I was so depressed that her efforts to uplift me emotionally were all in vain.

I continued attending the local school. The class teacher, Theopista Birwanya, was my cousin. Knowing that my brother had just died, she did everything possible to keep my spirits up at school. She encouraged me to play with other kids in the class during breaks to form new friendships.

By the time I started attending formal school at age five, I could recite the alphabet and count past fifty. My older brothers and sisters taught me the alphabet, counting, and simple arithmetic at home. I was more advanced in knowledge than most kids in the class. Because of their teaching, I used to score higher than most other kids in the class. At the end of the school term and school year, I always ranked either in first or second place overall in the class. The parents of other children in the class started complaining that the teacher, who was my cousin, was artificially inflating my grades. However, I never got any special instruction or coaching from her that other kids didn't get. The allegation that she gave me special favors or inflated grades was untrue. My better performance was due to the tutoring I was getting from my older brothers and sisters, which enabled me to grasp the concepts taught in class very fast. I could recite the alphabet and count out loud in class much better than other students.

Added to that, my father got two newspapers every day; one was Munno, and the other was Taifa Empya. He used to read the papers at the end of the day after he was finished with his daily work. Occasionally, he would hand me the newspaper and ask me to read it back to him. With the instructions I got from my older brothers and sisters, I could read a few words from the newspaper. My father also would ask me to listen to the evening news on the radio and go and tell him what was reported in the news. At that age, I could barely comprehend what was covered in the news, but I would try to tell him what I understood from what was said. All those tasks, however minor they may have been, made me a more advanced student at school and performed above my classmates.

In my second-grade year, when I was six years old, my parents arranged for me to go and live with my maternal uncle about 15 miles away. I didn't know exactly what the details were that led to my relocation. My uncle had a wife but had no children of their own. When I moved to his house, I was the only kid. After two years, my uncle brought my maternal cousin, a son, to his other sister to live with us. His name was Kamya, and he was three years older than me. With his arrival, I had someone to play with, which eliminated my loneliness. He joined the new school that I had been enrolled in. Because he was older, he knew more about life than I did. I was always willing to follow him around and learn more about life from him.

One day, while walking from school with my friend, I took a route that was not the usual route we always took home. We came across a mother duck with ducklings, and we chased after them, thinking that they were wild ducklings with no owner. We got hold of the ducklings and took them home with us. The duck's owner came home and found his ducklings missing. He found out that we had chased after and caught the ducklings. He came to our house to talk to my uncle. My uncle had never given me corporal punishment, but that night, I got a good beating. He said that he had to discipline me to ensure I didn't grow up to become a thief.

During school breaks, I would go back to spend time with my father, mother, and other siblings. Visiting back home with my parents and spending time and playing with my siblings was always an exciting time. They were older, and they treated me like a young kid. I didn't mind the attention.

At twelve, I was in seventh grade, a time when all students had to take an examination to exit the seven-year primary school education and start a four-year secondary school education. The school arranged for us to take the examinations in the capital city of Kampala. The school was located in the Mengo neighborhood next to a manmade lake known locally as "Kayanja ka Kabaka" (which translates as "King's Lake"). Legend has it that the King used to swim and fish in the lake. It is a man-made lake that was constructed around 1885 by King Mwanga II to connect his palace to Lake Victoria, also known as Lake Nalubaale. The king wanted to establish an escape route by water in case his palace was invaded.

It was my first time visiting the capital. With my classmates, I arrived at the city school months before taking the examinations. I spent some time taking classes at the new school. The excitement that I was attending a new school and was to take the exams in a city was unimaginable. We traveled on a public bus, and when we arrived in the city, we were housed within walking distance of the school. We walked to and from school in a group, and on the way back home in the afternoon, we would stop at the local market and buy snacks. Fried yucca root was my favorite snack.

I found the capital amazing since it was my first time to be in a place with so many people and so many vehicles. When the examination results were released, I had achieved a good grade. However, I was not accepted into the schools of my dreams. I was disappointed. I went back to my home district in Masaka to attend secondary school at a Catholic missionary school.

My father encouraged me to attend religious school. He was a religious man and the chief catechist of the parish. He was responsible for keeping the parish records. He would spend long hours every night working at his desk on parish records and correspondence. He also spent many afternoons visiting parishioners, helping them with their religious and spiritual needs.

## My Time At Masaka Secondary School

I spent a year at the missionary school, and while there, I never gave up my desire to attend the schools of my dreams. I worked hard on my studies to transfer to those schools. After one year of secondary education, I started applying to those schools for the transfer. One of them was a private missionary school, and the other was a public school run by the central government, and both were considered to be some of the best in the country.

I got invitations from both schools to take examinations with hundreds of other students from schools all over the country to compete for the open vacancies each school had. A few weeks later, I got a letter of admission to Masaka Secondary School in the center of Masaka city. I was thirteen years old, still young, and not capable of living by myself, so my parents had strong reservations about letting me move to the town and live by myself. They were leaning toward rejecting my move to transfer to the new school.

After days of convincing, my parents arranged for me to live with my cousin, who at the time had a job with an insurance company in the town. I lived with him and his wife and two children for one year. Unfortunately, my cousin tragically died in an accident on Easter night when his motorcycle collided with a car on a busy street in the center of the town. I was devastated.

On that night, my cousin was riding his motorcycle at about midnight to pick up his wife from her brother's house. I stayed home while he rode his motorcycle to his brother-in-law's house. An hour after he had left, his brother-in-law brought the wife home in his car. They asked me where my cousin was since they were waiting for him, and he did not show up. I told them that he had left to pick up his wife. Instantly, the wife said they had seen an accident involving a motorcycle in the center of the town. She started wondering if it was her husband who was involved in that accident. Without hesitation, we got into the car and drove back into the town center. Upon getting there, we saw the motorcycle and immediately recognized it was my cousin's bike. We were all distraught. I walked across the street to my cousin Theopista's home to let her know of the tragedy that had just happened. His body was still lying lifeless on the tarmac. The coroner picked up the body and took it to the mortuary. It lay in the mortuary for a week, after which it was transported to the ancestral burial place.

After his burial, my parents arranged for me to keep living with his widow as I went to school. The arrangement was temporary, and deep in my mind, I knew it would not be sustainable. I had three other cousins who lived in the town. They all were married and could not convince their husbands to let me live with them. The husbands were wealthy men who had successful careers and businesses but had their reasons for not allowing another person to live with them.

I quickly realized that I had to grow up fast; otherwise, I was not going to be able to continue with my education. I had to start taking charge of my life and be ready to live independently. I continued living with my deceased cousin's widow for a while. After three months, at the end of the school term, I found a studio room for rent. I talked to my parents and convinced them that I could take care of myself and could live alone.

Initially, they did not want to let me rent it by myself, so I had to do a lot of convincing. My maternal cousin, who was older than me, was attending Masaka Secondary School. I told my parents that the studio room I found was close to his and that if anything bad were to happen to me, he would be there to help me. They let me rent a room and for the first time, I was living by myself. The adverse circumstances following the death of my cousin forced me to become mature very early in life. I was paying rent and utilities, buying food, and preparing my own meals.

I continued to go to school, being a responsible student, attending all classes, and paying attention to schoolwork. I took my report card at the end of every school term and showed it to my parents to prove that I was indeed doing what I was supposed to be doing. I avoided any distractions that were ever present that came with urban living. Eventually, I graduated from Masaka Secondary School and got my Ordinary Level School Certificate awarded after twelve years of schooling.

During those years when I lived alone, I occasionally got some help from my three married cousins. I very rarely saw their husbands, probably because they were busy men. One was a district medical officer, the other was a district education officer, and the third was a businessman who had several agricultural processing plants.

Another person who played a role in my survival as a young teenager living alone was also a cousin brother. He worked in downtown Masaka but drove from my ancestral area to come to work in town. Occasionally, he would bring me bunches of bananas sent by my parents, and I would have plenty of food throughout the week. Learning from the generosity of my cousins and other relatives, I came to know that to succeed in life, one has to rely on other individuals. When I was financially able to help my other relatives, I took it as an honor to offer them help, mindful of what several people did for me when I was so young.

## Visiting My Brothers In Kampala City

During school breaks, I would travel to Kampala to visit my brothers. One of them taught at a college, and two others were elementary school teachers. The first time I visited them was an adventure for me. I saved my allowance money I used to get from my parents to pay for the journey. At the time, the taxi fare from Masaka to Kampala, eighty miles between, cost seven Uganda shillings. That was equivalent to one US dollar at the time. I had the fare and additional money that I could have used for unexpected emergencies during my travel. They had no prior knowledge of me going to visit them.

It was a sunny afternoon when I boarded a taxi from Masaka and headed toward Kampala on a mission to find my brothers. I had been to the capital city once before when I sat for my primary seven examinations at Mengo Primary School. I waved down a taxi traveling to Kampala, and the driver stopped. Other passengers were also traveling toward the capital city.

After I entered the vehicle, the driver asked everyone in the vehicle where they wanted to be dropped off. I told him that I wanted to get off at Kamengo Trading Center. I had never been to the trading center, but I knew that there were road signs identifying most trading centers. I had observed those signs before on my way to and from Kampala. I intended to stay attentive to spot those road signs and remind the taxi driver to drop me off.

I kept reading road signs as we traveled along the highway to locate Kamengo Trading Center. I, however, missed spotting the sign announcing arrival to Kamengo. It may have been damaged or removed. The taxi driver had forgotten that I was to be dropped off at Kamengo. I mistakenly trusted that he knew where I was to be dropped off. Many miles after we had driven past the trading center, the taxi driver asked me where I wanted to disembark. I told him that I wanted to get off at Kamengo Trading Center. By that time, we were ten miles past the location. We were in Mpigi Town. It was my first long-distance trip by myself.

The taxi driver stopped the vehicle by the side of the road as he was trying to figure out how he could get me back to Kamengo.

"Do you have the money to pay the taxi fare?" he asked me.

"Yes, I have the money," I replied.

"Do you have money to travel back to Kamengo?" He continued questioning me.

"I have enough money to take me back," I told him.

I was a student and did not have too much money with me. I had estimated that the money I had was sufficient for me to travel back to Masaka if any issues came up and I couldn't find my brothers. I was taking a calculated risk when I set off to travel. I had also set aside money to pay for a room in a motel for a night if I had failed to find a taxi to take me back to Masaka.

After stopping on the side of the highway for about fifteen minutes and trying to stop vehicles headed back in the direction of Kamengo, the taxi driver decided to drive to Mpigi Town. There was a taxi park in Mpigi Town where many of the taxi drivers stopped to pick up passengers. Once we got to the taxi park, he talked to several taxi drivers. Some of them seemed to be his friends. He asked them if they were driving toward Kamengo. He found one who offered to drive me back and also help me with finding my brother. He mentioned that he was a resident of the area and that he knew my brother. My brother taught one of his children at the local school.

I entered the taxi, and soon, we started traveling back to Kamengo. He drove to the trading center and dropped me off at a local store. He spoke to the store attendant to see if he could get me to my brother's house. The attendant said that he knew my brother, and he gave me directions on how to get to his house.

During that time of uncertainty, many thoughts were running through my mind, and at some point, I felt like I had hit a wall. I thought I would not be able to accomplish my dream of finding my brothers. I had seriously started to plan my trip back to Masaka city if I had failed to find them. My plan at that time was to board a taxi going in the direction I had come. I also thought of finding a motel where I could spend a night if I had failed to find a taxi back to Masaka.

While at the store, a customer came in to buy merchandise. After a brief verbal conversation with the store attendant, the customer ordered merchandise and paid for it. Then the store attendant asked him: "Do you know Emanuel?"

"Yes, I know him. He is my son's teacher at Kamengo Primary School," the shopper answered.

"This is his brother, and he is looking for him," the store attendant told the gentleman.

"Can you walk him to his house?" the store attendant asked the shopper.

"Yes, I can. In fact, I am going to pass by his house on my way back home."

The gentleman then told me to walk with him as he picked up the merchandise he had just paid for. I walked with him for about half a mile, and in no time, we reached my brother's house.

My brother was not expecting me, and he was very surprised to see me and wondered how I got there. By that time, it was approaching 7 p.m., and it was starting to get dark. I felt thankful to God for I had found my brother as I had started to wonder in the back of my mind what was going to happen if I didn't find him.

We stayed up late in the night talking. The following day, after he returned from his job, he showed me around the area. I stayed at my brother Emanuel's house for a week, after which I traveled with him to Kampala to visit my other two brothers, Peter and Joseph, who were residing in the capital. I had three weeks left on my school break by then. I split that time visiting the brothers, and both took time to show me around the city. Peter also took me on a tour of Nkumba College of Commerce, now known as Nkumba University, where he taught.

At the end of the school break, I took a taxi and traveled back to Masaka to continue with my education.

When school reopened, I was back attending classes and doing a lot of homework. Being busy with classwork, time went by very fast, and within a short time, the school quarter came to an end. I took my senior four examinations at the end of October and the first part of November. I knew that it would be close to five months before the results were released and selections for Advanced Secondary School began.

After taking the examinations, I traveled back to Kampala to be with my brothers. Five months was a long time for me to be sitting idle, doing nothing but waiting for the results of the examinations. Kampala was a much larger city than Masaka city, where I had spent years and where I had been forced by circumstances to turn into a grown-up in my tender teenage years and fend for myself. Those years had taught me many things and gave me the confidence to be and act independently.

I decided to go to my brother Joseph's house which was in Kololo neighborhood a few miles from Kampala city center. He had a government job after graduating from the University of Nairobi in the late 1960s. His job gave him exposure to business operators in the country and many people who run government agencies. He was also married to a woman related to one of the directors of the now-defunct East African Posts and Telecommunications Corporation, an entity that was set up and operated by the East African Community. Through my brother, I came to know which companies had job openings. I focused my job search on those companies, and I applied to no less than two companies every week.

Not long after I arrived in the city, I found work at the East African Posts and Telecommunications. In my lifetime, it was my second real job. I first earned a paycheck when I worked as an enumerator during a national census when I was thirteen years old. It was a two-day work, but I had to undergo training for days on how to conduct the count and fill out the enumeration forms. This time around, I worked for months, and I was paid well for someone with no prior experience. The East African Posts and Telecommunications' pay was higher than what Ugandan government departments and private companies in the country paid their employees. When I got my first paycheck, I bought a pair of shoes that were fashionable at that time. It was a high-heeled platform shoe that fitted well with my bell-bottom pants.

## My Time In High School

The job was only supposed to last me through the school's five-month break while I waited for the results of my senior four examinations. I had decided that I was going to go for further studies to get a high school diploma. Once the exam results were released, it was time to decide on a high school to attend. I was accepted at a high school located in the same neighborhood I lived in and was within walking distance from home. I could live with my brother and walk to school every day. It was a cheap way to get an education since I didn't have to pay for school dormitories. While working at my job, I made it a point to save money because I knew I would need it once I went back to school. Thus, some of the money I had saved from my employment went toward paying the tuition and buying school supplies. Throughout my two years of high school, I continued to live rent-free.

My brother had a maid who was a teenager close to my age. He had been working across the street from us but had decided to switch jobs and came to work at our home. During our conversation, he mentioned that he had to switch jobs because, at his former employer's house, there were adolescent girls. Their parents went to work and returned in the evening. The parents didn't feel comfortable leaving the male maid with the teenage girls all day while they went to work. They chose to hire a female maid and let go of the male maid. Luckily for him, that was the same time my brother was looking for a maid, so he quickly found a job.

When he came over to work for us, the children from his previous workplace occasionally came over to visit him. One of those kids was a teenage girl called Eva. She had discovered that we had a telephone in our house, and unlike the phone at her home, the phone in my home had no outgoing call restrictions. Rotary phones of those days could be locked to avoid being used by unauthorized people in the house to make calls. At my house, we could make calls as we pleased. Eva used to come over every so often in the afternoon, after school, to call her friends. I got to know Eva, and eventually, we became friends. I had seen her before playing in the street but had not talked to her. She was one of the young teenage girls who used to play on the street and frequently walked the streets in the neighborhood with her other friends. As years went by, we got to know each other very well. We used to walk together toward

Kampala downtown through the golf course that was two blocks from my house. Occasionally, we would sit under a tree on the golf course and spend time talking.

I lived in the Kololo neighborhood during the years of Idi Amin, the notorious dictator who is remembered for killing many of his fellow citizens and foreigners alike. He took power by military coup in 1971, and for eight years, until 1979, he and his henchmen terrorized the country. He had a residence in the Kololo neighborhood, very close to where I lived, and many of his generals lived in the neighborhood. As a teenager, I used to walk past their residences. Their bodyguards knew me and my friends as neighborhood kids, and they never gave us any trouble. Often, they would wave to us or try to strike up a conversation with us.

As a neighborhood kid, I knew all the undesignated walkways that I would use as shortcuts to go from one part of the neighborhood to the other. Many of those unofficial walkways went by Idi Amin's generals' residences or residences of foreign diplomats. There was not a single time that I was questioned by the soldiers who guarded the dignitaries' residences. I used to walk in the neighborhood after dark without ever thinking that I would be in trouble. Idi Amin's soldiers were feared for their cruelty, and very few people dared even drive or walk by his residence or the residences of his top generals.

There were nights when Eva spent days at her sister's house, who was living a few houses from Amin's residence, and I would escort her home. Our regular hangout place was the golf course that was a couple of blocks from where Eva and I used to live. Eva's residence was across the street from mine, and my bedroom faced her house, so I could see her from my bedroom window. I had come to know her routine; I knew that during weekdays, she would walk three blocks through the golf course to go meet her father.

It was always after I finished doing my homework and home study in the afternoon after school that I would walk with her through the golf course and occasionally spend time sitting and talking on the golf course. Ours was just a friendship with no romance involved. She was still too young and under observation by her relatives, and I was still young to be romantically involved with any girl.

I used to spend my evenings after school going to movie theaters or hanging out with my friends in the downtown area. I would hang out until around eight at night, and then I would walk back to Kololo in time for dinner. Eva and I did not start being romantically involved until I went to Makerere University as an undergraduate. We continued to see each other for most of the time I was at the university. She used to visit me on campus, to the disapproval of her brother, who also lived in Lumumba Hall, as I did.

Throughout my high school years, I put my heart and effort into getting into Makerere University. During those years, the country's economy was performing very badly. There were shortages of essential items throughout the country. My high school didn't have many reference books and other materials necessary for teaching. I, however, made it a point to look for reference books in many different places where I thought I could find the information I needed. In the afternoons after classes, I used to walk to Makerere University's main library to look for and read books with relevant information to what was being taught in our high school classes. The university let me use the library to read books even though I was not a university student. I could not check out the books. Those library books were a major part of why I was able to graduate from high school with good grades and be admitted to the university. Another reason is that all my high school teachers taught at the university and came to teach at my high school as a side hustle. They were well trained in educational instruction with vast knowledge of what they taught.

# Chapter 3

# After High School And Becoming An Adult

Two years of high school went by fast, and in no time, I had to take the high school exit examinations. Soon after taking the examinations, I found a job in a factory that manufactured facial and hand tissues, file binders, and a variety of other office stationery. I held that job throughout the seven-month school break as I waited for the high school examination results. It was a great job; I learned how to use machines in the factory within days. Having been the youngest and only student at the factory, my nickname was "School Boy." When the results of the high school examinations were released by the Ministry of Education, I had scored quite well.

Close to the end of the break, Makerere University, the country's only university at the time, released a list of students admitted to this highest institution of learning. The university announced that the list of admitted students was out for everyone to see. I went to the campus to check if my name was on the list, and it was. I was so excited, but even more excited were my family members.

I felt sadness in my heart because my admission to the university came after my father had passed. I imagined how my father would have felt to learn of my admission to the University because he always emphasized to me the importance of education. I spent days thinking of him. He had died on an

Easter weekend following complications resulting from surgery. Ironically, my cousin, who died in a motorcycle accident and whom I lived with while attending Masaka Secondary School, also died on an Easter weekend. For many years in my youthful years, during Easter holidays, I had memories and sorrow because of those two people who were influential in my life. Both of their deaths brought about abrupt and unexpected changes in my life.

## Attending Makerere University

In July 1976, I reported to the Makerere University campus to start my first year of undergraduate education. I was assigned to Lumumba Hall of Residence. I was given a room to share with another first-year student. It had two beds, two study desks, and two small clothes closets, one for each occupant. There was no additional space left to store personal items.

I was excited to join the university. It was a dream I had way before my teenage years and through high school, wanting to be like my elder brothers who had attended college. My high school friends and I used to refer to the University as the "hill" because the university was built on Makerere Hill, which is one of the seven hills that comprised the original boundaries of Kampala city. From my high school, I could look west and see the university campus sitting atop Makerere Hill. I was always inspired to study even harder to achieve my goal of one day attending that university.

While attending Masaka Secondary School, I was responsible for my well-being, budgeting for my housing expenses, food, and utilities. In high school, I was cared for by my brother, who took care of everything from food to utilities and paid for housing. My stay at the university fell in between those two situations. My food, room, and utilities were all covered by money provided through government sponsorship. The only money I had to spend was on incidentals, and even then, every semester, the university gave me an allowance to pay for the incidentals.

The time I spent at the university helped me grow even more into being a responsible individual, making my own decisions, whether good or bad. I was the sole individual responsible for the outcome of my decisions. Having lived by myself before high school and taking care of myself, I had a good idea of what I had to do to succeed at university. I attended classes and completed my assignments without fail. I knew how to handle money and the budget for money I received as an allowance every semester.

At the university, I made long-lasting friendships, and I started seeing the world as an adult. Lumumba Hall of Residence, to which I was assigned, had a reputation of being the most radical of all the halls on campus. It spearheaded many of the strikes that took place on campus. I reported to Lumumba Hall a week before school opened during what was called "Fresher's Week." On campus, all first-year students were referred to as freshers, and they always reported on campus early to familiarize themselves with the campus before classes began. When the continuing students returned to campus, it was routine for the returning students to give the freshers a hard time. The continuing students teased the first-year students throughout their first year.

The year started calmly with students attending classes and participating in campus and off-campus activities, such as sports. After two months, students staged a strike that was campuswide with the ring leaders residing in Lumumba Hall. Students boycotted classes, marched, and gathered in front of the main administrative building in the morning, soon after their breakfast.

It didn't take long before groups of soldiers from Idi Amin's army started arriving on the campus. The students were addressed by a representative of the army, who ordered them to disperse and return to their halls of residence immediately. The students did not oblige but instead continued to congregate in front of the main administrative building. Realizing that the students were not complying with the orders, the soldiers forcibly made the students disperse with sticks and guns.

As the evening approached, word went around campus that soldiers would be returning to campus at night to punish students for their involvement in the strike. That evening, I left campus and walked across town, through the golf course and residential neighborhoods, and went back to Kololo to my brother's house. As it turned out, I made a wise decision because that night, the soldiers returned and terrorized students in Lumumba Hall the entire night. My roommate, who stayed on campus that night, jumped from the third-floor window and broke his leg. He spent the remainder of the academic year in the hospital, treating his broken leg. Several students fled the country into exile after that incident.

Notwithstanding that unfortunate incident, the rest of my stay at the university was very pleasant and quite memorable. There were no other student strikes for the remaining three years I spent on campus. My friends and I formed a group of five individuals with a very close bond, and we referred to our group as the Council. We had brotherly ties that lasted throughout our college days and even after we left campus. Three of us ended up sharing a house after we got government jobs. Unfortunately, one of our group members was shot dead by Amin's soldiers, and that left a big hole in the group.

Although we were all always having fun on campus and liked to party, we were all good students, and we graduated with high honors degrees in our respective fields of study. That helped us to get selected for government jobs soon after we finished college classes. Initially, I worked with the City of Kampala's planning division. After a few months, I went to work with the government ministry of Local Government. I held that job for a year and a half. I was engaged in urban planning for municipalities throughout the country.

I was stationed in Kampala but made frequent trips to different parts of the country to visit municipalities in other districts of the country. I used to spend several days or weeks working with local municipal officials on a wide range of planning issues.

I dreaded traveling to the northern part of the country because the country was involved in a civil war at the time. We had to travel through a war zone, and we went with a military escort to provide security. The presence of the military escort did not give me any comfort or a sense of security, for I knew of several occasions when the military was overpowered by the rebel forces with disastrous results.

# Chapter 4

## Plotting To Leave The Country

Throughout the one-and-a-half years I spent working at the Ministry of Local Government, I was constantly looking for ways to leave the country, primarily to pursue further education. The country was experiencing political and security instability, with the military consuming a big part of the national budget. Educational institutions were not adequately funded to offer advanced degrees.

I knew right from the time I graduated that if I wanted to pursue further education, I was not going to get it in the country. I also knew that it was not going to be funded by the Ugandan government, which was struggling to fund even the most basic necessities for its citizens. I had to devise a strategy to get me out of the country to seek further education. So, I decided to start looking for foreign-published newspapers and magazines to search for any educational opportunities advertised. I spent a considerable amount of time browsing through magazines, newspapers, and other publications at foreign embassies. I also looked in anything I could find published by foreign organizations that I thought could have had any information about graduate education. I found many of the magazines in libraries at the university campus, foreign embassies, and at government ministries' headquarters.

It was also normal for scholarships to be announced over the national radio in a segment of the broadcast that was known as Special Announcements. I would make it a point to listen to those announcements every day to see if I could pick up information that could lead me in any way, shape, or form to an academic scholarship. I applied for every scholarship I came across, no matter what country offered it. I applied to study in Western Europe, Eastern Europe, Asia, Canada, and other African countries. I never heard back from many of the organizations after I submitted my application, and a few replied with negative news.

In 1981, positive responses from different organizations and countries started trickling in. I received positive news from Australia, Canada, Britain, Eastern European countries, and the United States. I took the news with great optimism but kept all the options open on all the applications because I knew that the process of getting a final offer of a scholarship was difficult and involved jumping over many hurdles. I had witnessed applicants who thought they had the scholarship only to lose the chance to go for further studies either due to politics in the government departments or from the very top of the national government. Top government ministers could use their positions to divert scholarships intended for one qualified individual to another person who often turned out to be their relative.

Deadlines drew very close for several of the scholarship offers that I was supposed to accept. I accepted a scholarship to study in Britain at Nottingham University and another scholarship to go to Australia. Within a few days, I got an invitation to go and interview for a scholarship offered by a United States government agency through the Africa-America Institute (AAI).

I had made it a daily ritual to listen to radio special announcements after the evening news. There were occasions, however, when I could not listen and, one night when I didn't, names were read for people selected to go and interview for scholarships in the United States. I was among those people invited for the interview. My friend and coworker Gilbert had listened that evening, and he had heard my name called.

When I went to the office the following morning, he said to me, "I heard your name being read over the radio public announcements last evening. They want you to go for a scholarship interview."

He, too, was looking for a scholarship to pursue an advanced degree. We frequently shared information on scholarships, and we would go to our department head to get his recommendation before we sent our applications out. I checked with the Ministry of Education to confirm that my name was called for the interview. The ministry staff confirmed that I was on the list, so I started preparing.

The interview was organized through the Ministry of Education coordinating with the United States Embassy in Uganda and the United States Aid for International Development. It was held at the Crested Towers building, which housed the Ministry of Education headquarters. I was interviewed by personnel from the US Embassy, USAID, and the Ministry of Education. They questioned me as to why I wanted to get further education and how that education and training would help the country. I was well prepared, and I had all the answers.

At the end of the interview, it was my turn to ask questions. I asked the interview panel, "When am I going to know the results of this interview?"

"The decision will be announced in less than two weeks," a Ugandan government official answered.

"Should I come to the Ministry of Education or the US Embassy to find out?" I asked.

"How did you find out about the interview invitation?" the Ministry of Education official shot back.

I responded that I heard an announcement over the radio. The interview panel members broke out into laughter. "Wait for a radio announcement," said the government official.

After the interview, I felt good about my performance. Many other people were interviewed, and in the back of my mind, I didn't think my chances of being picked were better than slim. This was primarily because I did not have anyone in the highest levels of government to push my application and advocate for me, which was a common practice then. So, I kept all the options on other scholarships open.

From the day I was interviewed, I never missed a day without listening to the radio evening public announcements. After about a week as I listened to the radio announcements at night, I heard my name being read. I was again asked to report to the Ministry of Education headquarters regarding a scholarship to the United States. Just for being called back to the Ministry of Education headquarters, I couldn't sleep all night, even though

I had no idea why I was being called back. My expectations were quite high that night.

I went back to the ministry, and I was notified that I was one of the people picked for the African Graduate Fellowship Program (AFGRAD) scholarships. The AFGRAD scholarships were offered by the US Government and administered through the United States Agency for International Development (USAID). The scholarship program covered the entire continent of Africa with applicants from all over the continent.

I had been selected for the scholarship and had started the hard work to meet a long list of requirements to get to the university I was to attend. I had been picked but I had no university admission yet. Before I could be admitted to any university in the United States, I had to pass aptitude tests that included the Graduate Record Examinations (GRE) and Test of English as a Foreign Language (TOEFL). The Ministry of Education gave me information on how to register for both tests. I took the tests in Kampala, and the results were sent to several universities in the United States.

Throughout that time, my apprehensions as to whether I would leave the country to further my education remained. The interview was held in March of 1981 with the anticipation that I would start in September of the same year. In August I was notified that due to budgetary constraints in the US, my start date had been moved into the following fiscal year. The US economy was going through an economic recession that extended well into 1982. Like the US government, universities were going through hard financial times and had set limits on admissions.

After I was informed that I was being processed for the 1982 scholarship offers, I felt like all my dreams had sunk to the bottom of the ocean. I knew that a year in Uganda at that time meant that things could turn out to be completely different. It could have been a new government in power with very different foreign policies. Or it could have been a change at the Ministry of Education where a new boss could have reversed decisions previously made. Even the head of the department in the local government ministry where I was working could have rescinded his endorsement for my scholarship. I spent months worrying, and I continued to submit scholarship applications to universities in other countries.

My worries worsened when, during that time, one of my coworkers told the head of my department that I had three scholarship offers. He asked the head of the department to rescind his approval of my scholarship application to the US. Luckily, the head of the department did not take his advice, and I continued with the process of fulfilling the scholarship requirements.

Several months after I took the aptitude tests, I got back my results of the GRE and TOEFL examinations. I scored well on the tests, which meant that my application would continue to be processed. In April of 1982, I received letters from the US stating that I had been admitted to the University of Washington in Seattle to start school in September of 1982. With that admission in hand, I continued working closely with the Ministry of Education to get a passport and arrange travel to the US. Getting a Uganda passport during that time was difficult; everyone who applied had to undergo extensive screening.

The scholarship offer required that I pay for my travel expenses and only start getting scholarship money after arriving in the US. Buying a ticket to the US was a big hurdle to overcome. Like other government ministries in the country, the Ministry of Education had a strained budget. Little money for travel expenses was available in the ministry's budget.

Months went by without me getting information about whether my application was advancing. By the middle of June, I made two weekly trips to the Ministry of Education to find out if there was any progress. In July, I made it a daily routine to stop by the Ministry of Education offices to ensure my papers were being processed. The office was within walking distance from my job, so I could leave my job and walk to the Crested Towers building.

August 1982, the month I was to travel to the US, was drawing near quickly. I started having sleepless nights, worrying if I would get money from the Ministry of Education to buy an air ticket. The cost of a return ticket was close to sixteen hundred dollars. I didn't have that kind of money. In addition to raising money for the air ticket, I would have had to raise money to pay for hotels on my way and other expenses.

Success in dealing with the Ministry of Education during those chaotic days in Ugandan government offices heavily depended on knowing someone in the office to act as your advocate. I approached my cousin, who worked for the Ministry of Education, for advice on what I should do to get funds for my air ticket and get a passport. He directed me to the right people to talk to in the Ministry.

Knowing the key people to contact helped me go through the process of getting the air ticket and travel allowance money to travel to New York. My worries subsided when I started to notice that I was making progress. It was common for people who had won scholarships to study abroad not to go to those destinations because their applications were not processed in a timely manner. I did not want to end up in the same boat, for I had worked so hard and gone through many emotions to achieve what I had thus far.

On one afternoon in August, I went to the Ministry of Education office, and I was informed that the Permanent Secretary had signed my vouchers to purchase an air ticket and another voucher for me to get money from the Bank of Uganda to cover my travel expenses on the way to the US. As a government employee, I had to get money equal to what the government policies allowed for employees of my level.

At the same time, I was handed my passport, which had been issued by the Ministry of Internal Affairs. I took my passport to the US Embassy to apply for a travel visa. I was to have a stopover in the United Kingdom, and I confirmed from the British Embassy that I did not need a visa for the stopover.

I dropped off the passport with proof of a return air ticket at the US Embassy in the morning and the staff told me to return in the afternoon to pick it up. I entered the embassy building, and I was briefly interviewed, after which I was handed my passport with a visa to enter the United States. It was at that moment that I believed that I was getting close to the end of my treacherous journey of searching for higher education. I went to my brother's office, which was located across the street from the US Embassy, and I told him that I had a visa and a voucher to take to the Bank of Uganda to get travel money. The following morning, I walked into the bank building and cashed in my travel allowance voucher. Instead of being handed American paper currency, I got traveler's checks that I had to convert into cash outside of the country.

## Preparing To Leave Uganda

It was the first week of August, and the deadline for me to travel to the US had drawn very close. With an air ticket and passport in hand, it was time to make specific and firm decisions about my journey and to say goodbyes to my relatives and friends. I had many thoughts running through my mind about how I was going to approach my graduate studies and how I was going to help the family I was leaving behind. I had one week left to prepare for the journey, to decide what to do with the possessions I had. By that time in my life, I had started accumulating personal items for use in the house, which I shared with my college friends. My girlfriend Eva used to spend time with me at the house, sometimes spending weeks with me. I knew that Eva would be going to live with her elder brother after I left. I had to choose from a long list of relatives whom to visit and say goodbye to and who to skip. My master's degree program was to last two years, and I was not going to see my family and friends for at least two years. I could not pay for the travel expenses.

I had many family members living in Masaka, including my mother. I was faced with a difficult decision during that last week of whether to risk my life to go say goodbye to her. At that time, because of the civil war, some parts of the country were under rebel forces' control and inaccessible. In 1981, a group of soldiers led by Yoweri Museveni chose to start fighting a guerrilla war after the highly controversial 1980 general elections that saw a former president, Milton Obote, being re-installed as president. By 1982, the rebel soldiers had control of much of the western and central area of the country, including Masaka.

Traveling to Masaka to say goodbye to my mother would have been a huge risk, for it would have meant crossing the frontline between the rebel fighters and the government soldiers. I kept imagining the joy I would have brought to my mother if I had been able to stand in front of her and say, "Mom, I'm going to America; what I had dreamed of all my life is finally happening."

I still had bad memories of a previous encounter with the army. In the first part of 1981, on a weekday morning, while I was walking along Buganda Road to my workplace, rebels fighting to overthrow the government attacked the ruling party's headquarters in the city center. I was less than half a mile from my apartment on Buganda Road. In search of the rebels, the army and the police rounded up people in the city and loaded them on trucks. I was one of those people rounded up, and I was transported to a police station.

For the entire day, the police interrogated us, wanting to know if we were part of the rebel group that attacked the Uganda People's Congress office building. I was held at the police station from seven thirty in the morning until seven o'clock in the evening. Some people were transported to the army barracks after the interrogation. I don't know what happened to them, but I was relieved that I was released. In those days, many people who were sent to military barracks ended up being killed.

My parents had before sent a son to study abroad; my brother studied at the University of Nairobi in Kenya. But still, I knew my mother would have been so excited to hear that I was traveling to the United States and going for a higher education, not just for touring. Unfortunately, I could not go and say goodbye to her. If I had decided to travel to see her, I would have risked not being able to return to Kampala. If I had gotten stuck in Masaka, it would have resulted in missing my travel to the United States. I discussed my dilemma with my brother Joseph, and we concluded that it was too risky for me to go to Masaka to say goodbye to my mother. It was a decision I made with great pain. I still feel a sense of guilt, thinking that I should have made that journey. I did not see her alive again; she died during my second year in the United States. I occasionally spoke to her over the phone, but that was not satisfying to me. My brothers and sisters would also update me over the phone on how she was doing.

I spent the entire second week of August 1982 making final preparations for my journey. I said goodbye to friends and family members who resided in Kampala. I packed my bags and cleaned up my work area at the Planning Department in Uganda House building. I still vividly recall a conversation I had with Mr. Lukambuzi, an older gentleman I used to sit next to in the office. He always acted as a father figure to me at work, advising me on a lot of life and work matters. He had come to know some of my family members, and I had gotten to know him. He asked me to keep in contact and look out for his son, who was also planning to travel to study in the United States.

# Chapter 5
## Travel to Entebbe Airport

My flight out of Uganda was scheduled for Thursday morning, August 1982. I flew out of Entebbe Airport and headed for Gatwick Airport in the United Kingdom. That morning, my brother came and picked me up from my apartment on Buganda Road and drove me to the airport. I was accompanied by a group of friends: my sister Mary, cousins Nora and Margret, and my girlfriend Eva. My brother's wife, Cissy, had just given birth a few days prior and could not make it to the airport.

After checking in at the terminal, we all hugged, and I proceeded to walk toward the gates to board the plane. My walk through the corridors of the airport building was not without incident. As I walked, I was stopped by one of the security personnel. He was standing in a corner that was not visible from the rest of the building.

"Where are you traveling to?" he asked.

"To the United Kingdom to take a flight to the United States," I answered.

"Do you have dollars, pounds, or any other foreign currency?" he asked me.

"I don't have any currency except Uganda shillings. All the money in foreign currency I have is in traveler's checks," I told him. I went on to explain to him that I was a government employee, and all my travel allowance was given to me in travelers' checks. He didn't believe me.

"You have to give me fifty dollars before I can let you proceed to board your plane," he said. "If you don't give me the money, you will miss your flight."

I pulled the travelers' checks out of my pocket, and I showed him what I had. They were in large amounts of one hundred. I insisted that I had no dollars, and I continued to tell him that I was a government employee and the government expected me to be in the US by Monday. He continued to hold me for about five minutes. Eventually, I convinced him that I was not going to give him any bribes and that his not letting me proceed to board the plane could have resulted in problems for him. He let me proceed to the gate.

The flight took off on time, as scheduled. I looked out of the window, and I saw people standing on the airport building balcony waving to the plane. I knew my friends and relatives were among those people waving. I especially thought of Eva, a person I had been friends with for almost ten years by then, longer than any of my other friends who came to see me off.

On the flight, I continued thinking of what I could do to help my family. Since my childhood, I had big dreams, and the major of them all was to go to the United States. It is a country I used to hear my parents talk about. Also, my uncle, who had fought overseas in the Second World War, used to talk about America a lot. The time on the flight was a time to reflect on all those dreams I had held in my head all my life. As young as

I was, and despite having older brothers and sisters, I felt like I had a responsibility toward my entire family to see that they lived a happy, decent, and successful life.

The eight-hour flight to Gatwick Airport had one stop in Brussels, but I did not disembark. On the flight, we were served lunch and snacks. I did not find the food served on the Uganda Airlines flight from Entebbe to London appetizing. Many of the dishes served were foreign to me, with a few exceptions, and they tasted unfamiliar. Between figuring out what choice of food was served on the plane and imagining what I should do once I landed at Gatwick Airport in London, I continued thinking of how I could help my family.

I was the second in the family to study abroad, but I was the first to go study in countries referred to as "advanced countries." Unlike today, when many people have relatives living all over the planet, during the early 1980s, very few people had relatives who lived in Europe or North America. When I told people that I was traveling to the US, the first question they would ask was if I knew anybody living in the US, Canada, or Europe. At that time, just knowing such a person would give one bragging rights and an illusion of being important.

So, there I was. I didn't know anybody living in such countries. The thoughts that ran through my mind on the flight were: *"How do I get my brothers and sisters into any of these countries?"* I did not have the slightest idea of how to achieve that goal, but somehow, in the back of my mind, I had a belief that I wanted it badly and that I would get it done.

The desire to help my family members go to those advanced countries to get an education influenced many of the actions I took once I got into the US. My determination to bring relatives into the US was central to my decision not to proceed with further studies at the University of Illinois, Champaign. In 1985, I applied and was admitted to the university's Graduate School of Architecture's two-year program. I chose not to go to that school because, at the time, I was processing an application for my sister to come study in the US. Her application was progressing well, and she was admitted to study at Shoreline Community College in Seattle. I knew that if I went to Illinois, her chances of coming to the US would be dead.

I talked to my friend at the University of Washington about my dilemma of choosing between my studies at the University of Illinois, Champaign, and helping my sister come over to the US. I decided against Illinois after my friend told me that if I went to Illinois, I would be like a lone person running a marathon, and I was the only one in the race. I had to bring some of my relatives to study in the US. The decision not to go to the University of Illinois, Champaign, was a major sacrifice for my family.

Before I left Uganda, the Ministry of Education had arranged for personnel at the Uganda Embassy in London to meet me at the airport. When I landed, I was met by a lady from the embassy who took me to the hotel where I spent the night. She advised me on how to get from the hotel to Heathrow Airport the following morning and what kind of transportation I could use without spending too much money.

I ordered dinner from the hotel kitchen and went to bed. In the morning, I checked my flight details to the United States and found out how to get to Heathrow Airport. Midmorning the following day I took a taxi from the hotel to the airport with enough time left before the flight to the US.

# Chapter 6
## Arrival At JFK Airport And My First Days In The USA

It was the night of August 15, 1982, at about 10:00 p.m. local time, that I arrived in the United States, landing at John F. Kennedy Airport in New York. Unlike my arrival at Gatwick Airport, I didn't have anyone waiting for me in New York. It was indeed a new experience finding my way around the airport.

When I visited the US Embassy before I left Kampala, I had a discussion with embassy personnel representing USAID in Uganda about my travel arrangements. We talked about whether I had ever traveled to the US or not. I had never been to New York, and there I was, getting ready for my journey to this mega city. The lady assured me that I would be all right once I got to New York. She briefly explained that transportation from the airport to the city center was rather easy to figure out. She explained that there were buses and taxis that I could use to get into the downtown area. She knew I was familiar with taxis and buses and how they operated in Uganda. She told me that it was not very different in New York. She advised me that the cheapest way to travel would be by bus, and she proceeded to give me the bus number to take from JFK Airport, and the stop at which I was to get off the bus in downtown New York. She further told me that the easiest way to tell drivers where I was going in New York was to tell them that I was going close to the United Nations building. From photographs, I knew what the United Nations headquarters building looked like so I would know when I had arrived at my destination.

I was to report to the Africa-America Institute office in New York as soon as I got to the United States. I was to give them a call before I got involved in any other activities. The instructions I was given at the US Embassy in Uganda were for me to head directly to the office of the Africa-America Institute (AAI), where I was to meet my African Graduate Fellowship Program (AFGRAD) director. I got to New York at night, and the AAI offices were closed. I could not call the office to announce my arrival, hence I waited until morning. The office was expecting my call since they had prior knowledge that I had landed in New York aboard a Pan-American flight from London.

It was dark and past midnight, and I was at a giant airport with the task of figuring out how to get myself into downtown New York. I walked to the ground transportation area and looked for hotels where I could spend the night until the following morning. I was going to be spending the travel allowance I got from the Ugandan government to pay for my hotel. After making several calls to different hotels, I decided against spending a night in a hotel. There were only a few hours left before dawn. I looked around the airport terminal, and I saw many people in the airport seats, sleeping and covered with blankets. Many of them were travelers and some were resting their heads on their luggage. I was convinced that even I, too, could do the same and sleep in those airport seats for the rest of the night.

I spent the night at JFK Airport, where I found comfort in the chairs. I found a seat that was long enough on which I lay down and rested my head on my little bag that had all my belongings. I spent most of the night awake. I could not sleep since I had slept most of the time I was on the flight from London. Plus, my body was still functioning in the Uganda time zone, where it was daytime. In the end, my decision not to spend a night in a hotel turned out to be a wise decision since I would have spent the whole night awake. The night went by very fast, and there was a lot of activity at the airport terminal, with every minute presenting something interesting to see.

At daybreak, I went into the restroom to wash my face, brush my teeth, and change clothes. I ate breakfast at the airport and waited for the AAI/AFGRAD offices to open at eight o'clock. It was time to leave the airport, go downtown, and report to the AFGRAD office. I called the office and let them know that I had arrived in the country and that they should expect me to be at the office that morning.

I went to the ground transportation area again to find transport downtown. I looked up the bus number that the US Embassy staff advised me to take downtown. I quickly realized that finding the bus number that would drop me off near the AAI office was going to be rather cumbersome. I had saved money by not paying for a hotel room, so I chose to look for a taxicab. I gave the taxi driver the address for the AFGRAD office and explained to him that the office was near the UN building. He told me that he knew where the UN building was and that he drives there very often.

When I called the AAI/AFGRAD office that morning to let them know I had arrived, the staff read the office address back to me, and I confirmed that it was the same address I had. As we drove from JFK Airport, I had a casual conversation with the taxi driver, asking me where I was from, and I told him. He continued being inquisitive, asking what I was here to do in the US. During the conversation, he told me that he, too, had immigrated to the US from the Caribbean and told me what his experience was like when he first came to this country. The longer we spoke, the more I felt comfortable talking to him and feeling assured that I would get safely to my destination. He showed me a few monuments in the city, telling me about some of the famous city bridges.

I did not take note of the time to see how long it took us to get from the airport to my destination. However, it seemed we took longer than I had expected based on the descriptions I heard from the lady at the US Embassy in Kampala. The taxi driver dropped me off in front of the AAI office, where they were expecting me. I paid him the taxi fare, and he wished me a good stay in the United States.

Talking to the AAI staff, they asked me how much I had paid for the taxi ride, and I told them. They all gasped saying that that was too much money to pay for the taxi fare from the airport. That is when I came to realize that the friendly taxi driver had overcharged me even though he showed the fare on the meter inside the vehicle. There was not much I could do; he had already left. He did not take the shortest route. I was, however, happy and relieved that I was finally at my destination in New York.

The AAI staff welcomed me to the US, and we spent time talking about my journey as we sipped coffee and pastries. After a while, we started talking serious stuff. We went over information about my scholarship and what the expectations were. It was difficult to follow all the details for a person who had just arrived in the country after traveling for three long days. I had jet lag as I had spent the night at the airport with little sleep. Still set on Uganda time, my body clock was ready for a good sleep as it was night in Uganda. I picked up a lot of printed information about the scholarship, knowing that once I was all settled in, I would read and get a good understanding of the scholarship requirements. We talked about money matters, and the lady explained that my allowance would be paid at the beginning of the month and no later than the fifth of the month to enable me to pay my rent.

I was to find my own accommodation off campus. To start, I got a lump sum that was equivalent to a three-month allowance. In the beginning, expenses were expected to be higher, especially since I was new in the country. By then, I had more dollars on me than I had ever had in my life. I had also cashed some of my traveler's checks that I got from Uganda. The AAI staff advised me to open a checking account at a local bank once I got to Seattle to be able to cash my monthly allowance checks.

While at the AAI office, I learned that the program director had arranged for me to stay in New York for a week. The staff told me that they had arranged for a hotel room in the city, and they gave me the address. The lady said that I could take a taxicab to the hotel, and she told me how much it might cost to get there. Realizing that it might be difficult for me to get a taxi to stop and pick me up, she stepped on the street and called the taxicab. The driver showed up in a short time and the lady told him the hotel where I was going.

At the hotel, I identified myself and got the keys to my room. It was time to get some well-deserved rest. The AAI staff wisely scheduled a week for me in New York City. At the end of the week, I was rested and overcame jet lag. My body had adjusted to a new time zone. My responsibility was to call the AAI/AFGRAD program staff assigned to me to let them know when I was getting ready to leave New York.

My stay in the city was memorable as I got to see some famous sites and I attended a concert. I finally was in New York City, and I was enjoying every bit of it. I, however, was bothered by the weather, which was extremely humid and hot. It was a lot hotter and more humid than the weather I was used to in Uganda.

When I went to the restaurant, I repeatedly asked the waiter to re-fill my glass with water. I was so thirsty that I kept gulping the water down my throat every time the glass was filled. Eventually, I realized that the waiter had got fed up with me. I asked for a refill, and he just ignored me. I went back to my room and looked at the map to figure out where the closest store was located. Once I located one, I went and bought several water bottles that I kept drinking all night in my room. It was very different weather than I was used to in Uganda.

When it was time to travel to Washington, DC, I called the AAI/AFGRAD office and told them that I was leaving. I again arranged taxicab travel to the airport by myself. The difference this time was that I had a good idea of what it would cost to get to JFK Airport.

I arrived at the airport early for my flight. I had already contacted the Uganda Embassy in DC to let them know that I was on the way. I was required to go to the embassy and meet the education attaché as part of my travel. The original arrangement was for me to spend at least a month in Washington, D.C., attending English classes at George Washington University. I found out that AAI had arrangements for its students to take classes at George Washington University to brush up on their English language. While in New York, I was informed that I did not have to spend a month in DC taking the classes. The University of Washington I was going to attend had decided that I had scored high enough on my TOEFL examination and did not need to take any remedial English classes.

On a cool morning, I left my hotel room and walked to the Uganda Embassy to meet the education attaché. We talked about a range of topics, but the most important for me at that time was to know how to connect with my countrymen who were residing in the country. I needed to know if there were Ugandan students in Seattle where I was going to spend at least two years studying. I learned that a Ugandan pastor named Mr. Lukyamuzi was living about twenty miles from the University of Washington campus. The attaché gave me his phone number so I could contact him after I had arrived in Seattle. I learned that there were no students from my country at the university. I knew there was one student at the university from

Ghana who was being sponsored by the Africa-America Institute, which was the same organization that was sponsoring me. The AAI office had notified me about him while I was in New York and advised me to contact the foreign student office on campus to get connected with him.

I spent fewer days in Washington, D.C., than in New York, so I packed sightseeing opportunities into the limited time I had. I visited several monuments in the city and some important government sites. I decided to spend time walking around the city as much as I could. So, when I had to go to the Embassy for my meeting, I walked the distance while I admired the various structures and monuments.

## Traveling To Seattle

My flight to Seattle was in the evening, with a stopover in New Orleans. I arrived at Seattle Tacoma Airport at night. Instead of spending a night at the airport as I did at JFK Airport, I decided to get hotel accommodation. I knew more about how to get a hotel room, and I knew that I could ask the hotel to send a shuttle to pick me up from the airport. That is exactly what I did and within less than thirty minutes after I made a phone call to the hotel, I was picked up by the hotel shuttle.

The following morning, I made a phone call to the Ugandan pastor whose name and phone number were given to me by the staff of the Uganda Embassy in Washington, DC. I introduced myself to him and we chatted for some time, getting to know a little about each other. He inquired how I got his phone number, and I told him that I got it from the Uganda

Embassy staff. I told him how I was heading to the University of Washington campus and that I was going to attend classes at the university for two years. I gave him the hotel address where I had spent the night. He came and picked me up from the hotel and drove me to his residence.

We had lunch with his family, and we continued to get to know each other for the rest of the afternoon. We talked about where I was going to be living and if I was to be living in campus housing while I was going to school. By that time, I did not have much information about housing availability, but I knew that I had to find somewhere to live, no matter the circumstances. I was ready to use the adventurous skills that I acquired in my teenage years when I had to live by myself.

We then talked about where I was going to spend the night and the days before I started attending classes. I did not have a hotel to spend a night in, but I had decided that I was not going to spend money on fancy hotels. Instead, I was to find cheap accommodation to save money. I knew that the Young Men's Christian Association (YMCA) had rentable rooms at a reasonable cost that catered to people who were watching what they were spending on accommodation.

While still at the hotel at the airport, I called the YMCA in downtown Seattle and inquired if they had rooms available for rent, and they told me that they did. I made a reservation to spend days at the YMCA in downtown Seattle even before I left the hotel. So, when Mr. Lukyamuzi asked me where I was going to spend the night, I told him I was going to spend a week at the YMCA. Later in the evening that day, he drove me to the YMCA having hosted me as his guest for a whole day.

He waited in his car outside, making sure that I checked in before he left.

The room at the YMCA was perfect for me because, by then, I was spending my money like a student. I had shifted my spending to that of a student away from that of a paid government employee. There were no meals at the YMCA, and I had to walk out of the building to find restaurants nearby. Many of the meals I ate were cold sandwiches, which I bought from a convenience store located nearby in the downtown area.

I spent five days in the downtown area, and I used that time to find out where the University of Washington (UW) campus was located and how to get there. I made several trips to the campus after finding the bus routes that could get me there. I visited the admissions office to notify them that I was in town. From there I went to the international students' office to also let them know that I had arrived. In the paperwork instructions the university had sent me, they suggested that I go to the international students' office as soon as I got on campus. It was a good place to look for cheap housing near campus because many landlords with student housing placed advertisements in that office. The office also had information on how to navigate events on campus once classes started.

The International Students Office had many resources, and it provided me with a lot of useful information to help me establish myself not only on campus but also in the US. I now have a son in college who works with international students, helping them to get established in this country. He asked me what it was like to be new in a country, and talking to him reminded me much of what it was like for me to visit and work with the international students' office.

The office had a great deal of resources that international students could tap into to establish themselves. On a wall in the office, there was a board on which landlords advertised available rental units. That is where I looked and found my first rental room within walkable distance of the College of Architecture and Urban Planning, where I was to attend classes.

The owner rented out rooms in the house, and the tenants shared a kitchen and living room. Three other individuals lived in the house, and each of us made our meals. I rarely saw the other tenants since they came back home late at night.

The UW international students' office operated a "Host Family Program." The program connected new foreign students with families in the area interested in helping them establish themselves on and off campus. Those host parents showed the new students around town, including supermarkets, stores, places of worship, movie theaters, sports stadiums, and many other places a new student would need to enjoy their stay on campus.

The office introduced me to a couple that was living close to campus to act as my host family. The gentleman was a professor who had traveled and taught at Universities in Africa and had visited Uganda as a tourist. After years in Africa, he returned to the United States and settled into a teaching profession at the University of Washington. The wife was a stay-at-home mom, and the couple had two teenage boys.

The family was of tremendous help to me during my first days in Seattle. They took me to places where I bought basic necessities at very reasonable prices. They steered me away from places where I could have spent my money buying expensive items that were not necessary at that time of my life. I did not know the city, and I had no vehicle to drive to stores. So, my option during my first days in the country would have been to buy expensive things from nearby stores. The host family drove me around and advised me to stay away from the expensive stores. They took me to discount stores to buy pots, pans, plates, utensils, bedding, etc., all the things that I would not have been able to find on my own at a reasonable price.

After a month of living in the shared house, I ran into Victor, a student from Ghana who was also being sponsored by the AAI on the AFGRAD program. He is the AFGRAD-sponsored student that the AAI office in New York told me about. The AAI office did not give me his contact information and promised that they would let him know about me.

One morning, I was in a bank, opening an account, and I was struggling to understand the bank teller's accent. Victor walked to me at the bank counter and asked if I needed help with opening the account. He helped me with the bank procedures, after which he stayed, and we started talking. I found out he was a Ph.D. student, but most importantly, he told me that he was an AAI/AFGRAD-sponsored student. We connected instantly since we had something in common. Talking to him I got to learn more about how the AFGRAD program worked and how to navigate the program's requirements. I also learned that he had the same host family as the one I had been assigned to.

In the bank account I opened, I deposited my check for the first monthly allowance by AAI. I was fortunate to have met Victor because after talking to him for a while, I got to learn that the shared housing I was renting was not suitable for students. Victor advised me to look for particular types of rental buildings that were listed in the foreign student office as student housing. When I went back to the foreign student office, I got addresses for several buildings that were advertised as student housing. After several calls to the owners, I settled on one that was just blocks off campus, and I rented a room. It was a much nicer room with a television and study table and other amenities like a bookcase, and furniture items that are necessary for studying. I moved into that building with help from Victor and from then we remained good friends. From him, I got more helpful tips on how to live in the US and how to succeed as a student.

## Writing Back Home

It was the middle of the fall quarter, and I was completely immersed in classes and figuring out my new environment. For the first time in my life, I was experiencing cooler weather with temperatures below eighty degrees Fahrenheit. Prior to that time, I had only lived in Uganda, a country with warm weather all year round. I bought heavy jackets for the cold weather, and my body started getting used to the cold.

As I sat in classes and on some occasions, I would find it hard to focus on what was going on in the classroom. The classrooms were cold, and I felt homesick, missing my family and friends I had left back home. The days started getting shorter, and by the time I would get out of my classes and library, it would be dark, but the time was only five o'clock. At five o'clock in Uganda, there would be an additional one hour of sunlight.

One dark evening after I completed my homework assignments, I went out in the cold looking for a telephone callbox to make a phone call to talk to my relatives in Kampala. There were numerous telephone callboxes on campus and the task I had at that time was to locate them in the dark on a campus that I was still getting familiar with. I wanted to talk to my relatives and let them know that I was okay and started my classes at the University of Washington.

I had collected a handful of coins over some time that I was to use to make the call to Uganda. I entered a well-lit phone booth; I picked up the phone and dialed zero to get to the telephone operator. Once she answered, I told her that I was making a phone call to Kampala, Uganda. The US phone operator had to contact the operator in Uganda, who in turn had to connect me to my family member's phone line. After several tries, the call connection was unsuccessful. I had tried on several consecutive nights without success. In the early nineteen eighties, telephone communications between the US and Uganda were bad. The telecommunications infrastructure had been decimated during the wars that were being fought in Uganda. Getting a connection to the country's telephones was difficult.

Making phone calls was expensive for me, and I could afford to call only a few times. I eventually gave up on making phone calls to communicate with my relatives and reverted to writing letters instead. I bought several airmail sheets from the university bookstore, which was the standard for writing and sending mail overseas by then.

Airmail was written on very light, flimsy blue sheets with dotted lines along the ends marking how to fold and seal the letter before mailing. No stamps were required since the price of the airmail included postage. A sealed airmail could be dropped off at the post office without additional costs.

Once I sent the airmail, it took three weeks for it to travel from Seattle to Kampala. So, I waited, waited, and waited to hear back. The mail sent from Uganda took even longer to get to Seattle. It was like an eternity. After three months of waiting to hear back, I received a letter from my brother on airmail paper.

He expressed pleasure that I had gotten to my university destination without major issues and that I was doing well. He briefed me about the condition of my mother, who at that time was sick. He informed me that she was very worried, thinking that maybe I never got to where I was supposed to attend school. Having been a parent myself today and having sent my children off to school for the first time, I can understand why my mother was worried about me and why she had some sleepless nights. When I put my son on a plane to travel to Ohio to attend school, I was worried for days about him. Even when I sent my daughters to in-state schools, I was concerned about them every time they left home to drive to school for the first few weeks.

Even though it was tedious and costly to get a phone connection to talk to my relatives, I did not give up. During the school break, I spent time trying to get a phone connection at the telephone call box. I finally was able to connect with my brother and other family members. We were all excited to talk to each other although it was for a short time because the calls were expensive.

We mostly communicated by mail, and I wrote to them about life in America, the country that I had started to explore. I wrote about the many cultures and people in the US and my studies at the university. I told them how America had people from many other countries. I mentioned how I had met people from almost all corners of the globe. I described their material possessions and the people's behaviors. I talked about things people did that would be considered an abomination in Uganda.

For sure the differences between the Uganda culture that I grew up in and the cultures that I found myself surrounded with in the US were tremendous. In the letters, I narrated things that I thought were unimaginable in the Ugandan culture, such as seeing a man in the kitchen preparing lunch or dinner while the wife was relaxing on the couch. Growing up in Uganda, I never saw married men stepping into the kitchen to cook while the wife sat by relaxing.

Up to now, men who come to visit me here in the US from Uganda find it strange to see men cooking meals, just as

I was shocked when I arrived in this country. Different people, different cultures.

As I spent more time in this country and got to visit different places in Seattle, I encountered many other strange things that people did. I was surprised when I first saw a man carrying a baby while walking with his wife. In Ugandan culture carrying and caring for babies is done by women. So, when I spotted a man carrying a baby walking with his wife by his side, I took a picture from a distance, developed it, and sent it to my brothers for them to see for themselves. Now that I have lived in this country for decades, such actions don't even register in my mind when I encounter them. I carried my children when they were little, and I did not feel like I was doing something extraordinary.

I was cooking meals for myself, something you don't find many men do in Uganda. In this area, though, I had prior experience from my early years. While attending secondary school and before high school, I lived by myself and made meals for myself. I was not so much into cultural shock in that regard. My host family, who had lived in Africa, were familiar with my culture, and at one time, they asked if I knew how to make meals. I told them how I had cooked for myself before. The challenge for me, though, was learning to prepare meals with the ingredients found here in the US, which were different from what I was used to. They gave me a quick demonstration on how to cook spaghetti and jokingly told me that if I wanted to find out if the spaghetti I was cooking was ready, I could throw a strand on the wall. If the strand stuck on the wall, then the spaghetti was ready to eat.

There were times when I imagined what the situation would have been if I were in Uganda. Most likely, I would have hired a maid to cook for me and do all the housework since I had graduated from university and had a job. That is the norm in Uganda.

It is cheap to hire housemaids to do such work in Uganda. Living in America, it was impossible to afford a maid to cook and do my housework. It was not something that I could even have dreamed of. I was living on a student allowance that went toward rent and food. With a maid, I wouldn't even have had money left over to buy food. Labor is expensive in this country. I believe that those men who visit here and get bewildered to see men cooking would instantly change their minds about men cooking. Economic circumstances in this country can't support Uganda's cultural beliefs and traditions.

# Chapter 7
## Settling In At The University Of Washington

I arrived in Seattle in August 1982, so I had a whole month to settle in and get ready for school to start at the end of September. By Christmas time, I had completed my first quarter at school. It was my first Christmas away from my family for the first time in my life, and I felt lonely, missing the family gatherings I was used to.

During the school quarter, I had to adapt to a new way of learning and class instruction. I was in graduate school, and learning meant taking personal initiative to research and learn what I needed to know. The professors were facilitators who helped guide me through the learning process. They would offer guidance but would not spoon-feed me with information. Much of the learning was through personal research, observation, and making conclusions from the information I gathered. Graduate school education is meant to make you question what is generally considered to be established truth. It teaches you to ask the why, how, when, and what-if questions. I learned not to believe everything I heard or read and to look for facts in every statement. It was helpful that during my undergraduate education at Makerere University, I was required to write a research paper to graduate. I did all the research myself, wrote a thesis, and defended it before a panel of professors, some of whom were from universities abroad. I used that research background to my benefit at the University of Washington.

During the second quarter, I had to register for urban design studios and research seminars. One requirement in those classes was to form a study group. We were to choose a topic of study, form a research framework, do the research, and present our work at the end of the academic quarter. Forming a team had many advantages, as it prepared me for what I encountered when I entered the workforce after graduation.

I was the only black student in the class which presented hurdles for me as someone new in the country and very unfamiliar with the culture. Trying to form a group put before me what racism and other forms of discrimination were about. While growing up in Uganda, I did not experience much discrimination. I was part of the majority tribal group, the Baganda, and if I wanted, I could have avoided people who treated me differently because of who I was. I did not have that luxury here in the US, where I found myself the only black person in the class, and I had to accept it as a fact.

I noticed that whenever I tried to team up with individuals, they would leave, and I would be left standing there by myself. The other students I was trying to team up with would walk away, coming up with excuses, while others gave no excuses. This is something that happened to me many times. People tended to form teams with their racial groups. Asians teamed up with Asians, whites with whites, and Arabs with Arabs. So, my challenge was to figure out how to meet the class requirements where the work had to be done in teams and when no team would let me join them.

Noticing that students were forming groups with their kind, the professor set a requirement that teams be of people from different backgrounds. The backgrounds had to be based on their prior field of education, past work experience, or the classes students were enrolled in during that quarter. The professor had everyone introduce themselves to the entire class and say what their backgrounds were. The professor then made suggestions as to who should team up with whom to have diversity on teams. I teamed up with an Asian student and an American white student. We spent the entire quarter working on the urban design studio project. We came up with planning and design recommendations on how to improve livability standards and lifestyle in the study area that was developed with homes built in the late 1800s and early 1900s.

Forming our diverse team turned out to be a good educational experience. In addition to learning and producing a report required of us to pass the class, we got to learn and understand each other's cultures. The classmate from China had never closely interacted with a black person. During my education in Uganda, I had frequent interactions with South Asian students and white educators. Working very closely with my Chinese and American white classmates almost daily for an entire quarter gave me a deeper insight into the Chinese and American cultures. The Asian classmate seemed to take great interest in examining my black skin, trying to figure out what becomes of it under different circumstances. He was amused by the ashy appearance of my skin once I took a shower and did not apply lotion. Some individuals would have negatively thought of such an inquisition, but I had got to know my classmate and I understood that he had no bad intentions or feelings. Rather, he was trying to learn about something that he had never come across in his life.

The longer we spent time together in groups, the more we came to realize that our cultures, though they seemed to be different, had many similarities. Each culture has likes and dislikes. No one culture liked or disliked everything they came across.

The following winter quarter, I again teamed up with my white American classmate in yet another design studio. By then, we had become good friends, hanging out together even outside of class hours. Our professors continued to emphasize the need to form teams and especially to team up with people from backgrounds other than ours. They emphasized that being in college offers an exceptional opportunity to get to know other cultures and people without additional cost other than the tuition paid. It was the best way to introduce us to what we were to encounter in workplaces once we graduated. Many jobs require teamwork, and in many instances, the job does not give the luxury of picking who to team up with. That rendered true to the saying that "college is a learning experience."

College puts you in contact with people from different parts of the world and cultures. After three academic quarters, we all socialized with each other, and our cultural differences were no longer a hindrance to working together on class projects. We had become comfortable with each other regardless of race, skin color, and country of origin.

In 1985, I was in the final year of my study at the University of Washington, and I knew that my visa to stay in the US was expiring by the end of the school year. There was a possibility that I would not be allowed to remain in the US after I completed my courses; I had to have an alternate plan B. Alongside the idea of bringing my relatives to the US, I had thoughts of what I would do if I had been forced to go back to Uganda.

I was determined not to leave this country the way I came, with nothing. Neither did I want to return to Uganda and live the same life I lived before. So, my thoughts were running wild. I saved some of the money I received from my scholarship monthly allowance and from the campus jobs I worked while I went to school. My goal was to buy items I could use if I were to return to Uganda. I had plans to buy a car and send it by ship, plus household appliances, furniture, and nice clothes. I was never going back to living the same lifestyle I had lived before 1982.

# Chapter 8
# Employment At The City Of Seattle And Tukwila

At the end of the Spring quarter in 1985, I found a job advertisement at the university campus for an internship position with the City of Seattle. The position was in the Planning and Engineering Section of the Park and Recreation Department. I applied for the position, and I was invited for an interview at the Human Resources Department office in downtown Seattle. After the interview and positive recommendations from my professors, I was offered the job. I was asked to report to the Parks Department office located close to the Space Needle. I started working as a municipal intern, producing drawings to revamp the city's parks that were being renovated. I would spend all day producing drawings, and at the end of the assignment, I had prepared drawings for all of the parks in the city. Occasionally, I would get out of the office and visit parks to assess the condition of the park or the play equipment.

It was a fun job because it involved drawing plans which I enjoyed doing, putting my drafting and design skills to work. The work was intended to last for three months, ending in the fall with the start of the school year. The duration was extended, and I ended up working with the city for over a year. At the end of the assignment, I updated my resume and started looking for a job. The internship had given me work experience to put on my resume, in addition to education. I had come to learn that the experience I had attained working in Uganda was not valued as being useful here in the US. The times I included that work experience resulted in more questions from the interviewer, some of them not related in any way to the job I was interviewing for.

My job search strategy was to draw up a list of companies each day and visit every one of them, talk to the individuals at the company about work opportunities, and leave my resume. After a week I would go back and check with each of the companies to see if my resume had been reviewed and if they had any job in the company that could utilize my skills and experience. From some companies, I got the news that they would have openings soon. I would offer to do volunteer work for free in the office since that was a frequent way many people landed jobs in those days. The strategy was that if I volunteered at the company, once the position opened, I would apply for it and interview with sufficient knowledge of the company. That would give me a leg up. Between 1985 and 1986, the Seattle metropolitan area was going through an economic downturn, and jobs were scarce. The major employer in the area was Boeing, and the company was cutting jobs at its manufacturing plants. Through a multiplier effect, those layoffs ended up negatively affecting other sectors, which in turn resulted in employers cutting jobs.

I was interviewed several times, and I was competing with people who had more years of experience and had been laid off during the recession. Jobs were being offered to people with more experience. That did not deter me or diminish my determination to find work. I frequently went to the University of Washington campus to check the various bulletin boards that were scattered all over campus to see if there were jobs advertised. The few jobs that were advertised at that time were for students who were actively enrolled in classes. I had completed my studies by the fall of 1985 and officially graduated even though I could have registered for classes. I had completed all my required classes, and my thesis had been certified; thus, I had satisfied the graduation requirements. That disqualified me from many jobs advertised on campus.

Several months went by without a job until the first part of 1986, when a job was advertised at the City of Tukwila for a Planning Intern. It was open to those who had an education in planning and/or architecture and did not require applicants to be enrolled in school. The job did perfectly fit my qualifications because I had a background in planning, urban design, and architecture. I applied and was invited for an interview, and I was offered the position.

The City of Tukwila is located 10 miles south of the City of Seattle along Interstate Highway Five to Oregon. I had to wake up early every morning, much earlier than when I was working in the City of Seattle, to navigate the heavy morning traffic that I usually encountered on the I-5 Highway South.

The City of Tukwila's economic existence was supported by a giant regional shopping mall that attracted people from many miles away. In 1986, the city was working to bring in other types of uses to complement the mall's existence. Attracting housing and manufacturing activities was top of the list. My work assignment was focused on planning and developing policies necessary to achieve the goal of diversifying the

City's land use and tax base. Those job assignments were different than the work I did at the City of Seattle, where I spent most of my time generating park drawings. This new job introduced me to aspects of long-range planning, and I was able to put into practice what I learned in class and urban design studios.

While interning at the City of Tukwila, I continued to search and apply for jobs, focusing on getting a permanent job that had benefits, like paid insurance and retirement. It was a tall order in the Seattle metro area at that time since most employers did not want to hire people for long-term assignments. The economy of the area was losing jobs. I therefore decided to expand my search area, and I started looking for jobs in other states to the south of Washington state. Oregon and California are the states I focused on.

The jobs were advertised in printed newspapers and magazines. The newspapers were from different states, and most jobs were advertised in the Sunday paper. Every Tuesday and Wednesday evening, I would go to the University of Washington's Suzzallo Library newspaper section, pull out several Sunday newspapers, and spend hours looking for jobs. I would write down the jobs that interested me for that week, and I would make phone calls to request applications. During those days, the convenience of searching and applying for jobs on the Internet did not exist. All applications were completed with a pen and paper and mailed through regular postal mail.

There was also Jobs Available, a publication that came out every month and advertised jobs available in all fifty states and the District of Columbia. The publication grouped jobs by profession, and at times, the book would be over one hundred pages.

As I spent time looking, I realized that California had many more advertisements than Oregon. I, therefore, narrowed down my search area and was razor-focused on California. The Los Angeles Times used to have several pages of job advertisements, all well arranged by profession. So, I would quickly turn to a page that advertised jobs in areas I wanted: planning, urban design, and architecture. The LA Times advertised jobs not only in the Southern California area but the entire state including northern and central California. It was a gold mine when it came to jobs.

I applied for jobs all over California, and I was ready to relocate from the Seattle area, where I did not see an end to the job recession that had hit the area. Most jobs in California made it clear that they didn't pay for relocation. I was willing to pay for my relocation. I devised a system of collecting information on employers, and soon, I had a notebook full of employer names, phone numbers, and addresses. Next to each entry was a space where I made notes about the employer, the date I sent an application and resume when I followed up, and the comments I got back. I arranged it in a manner that it was easy to read and to quickly decide on what action to take next.

The Southern California region at the time was booming with economic activity. The area had a concentration of high-paying defense jobs, including airplane and weapons manufacturing. The cold war between the US and Russia was escalating to greater heights. President Ronald Reagan had decided to spend more money on defense weapons. The abundance of defense, construction, and weapons manufacturing jobs meant that there were sufficient high-income earners who were willing to spend money in the area. That led to expansion in other sectors of the economy, and thus, more jobs were created that did not directly employ defense industry workers.

Weeks went by, and I got an invitation to interview for an entry-planning position with the City of Burbank. I bought an air ticket from Seattle to Los Angeles International Airport. I spent a night in Burbank, and the following day, I went to the interview. It was held in the afternoon, and afterward, I spent time sightseeing in Hollywood. The following morning, I took a taxicab to the airport and flew back to Seattle Tacoma Airport.

After spending a couple of weeks waiting for a response, I called the Burbank Human Resources Department and asked how far along they had advanced with the selection process. I was disappointed when the clerk told me that my name was not on the list of those chosen to continue with the interview process.

After this interview, I had a discussion with a couple of my friends about the results of my interview in California. I told them how I got rejections from the two employers so far. They suggested that I should not waste money flying into California for job interviews and that I should instead only go to interviews in nearby cities. The problem, though, was that it was hard to get interviews for jobs in the Seattle area. I was forthcoming with them and told them that I was going to continue sending applications to California. It was fertile land when it came to jobs.

So, I continued going to Suzzallo Library to search through newspapers and review advertisements in the Jobs Available publication. I sent out applications, including one to the County of Riverside for the job they advertised in the Los Angeles Times newspaper. At the same time, I applied for a job and got an interview invitation for a job in central California. I did not go to that interview primarily because the place was not easy to reach. I would have flown into San Francisco and taken a long drive by road to the interview.

Working at Tukwila, I had started getting comfortable in the job when I received a response from the County of Riverside to interview for a planner position. The invitation asked that I call to confirm that I would attend the interview, which I did. My next task was to ask and convince my supervisor at the City of Tukwila to get time off to travel to California. I put in my request, and it was approved. I did not mention to the supervisor that I was traveling for a job interview or that I was going to fly to California.

I booked a flight to Ontario, California, again, flying out of Seattle-Tacoma airport. After landing at Ontario Airport, I took a bus to downtown Riverside and started looking for a motel to stay at. I spent some time checking out motel rates by going from one motel to another, and I finally spent a night at one that offered the cheapest rates but looked decent. I had spent money prior without getting positive results from the interview, so I was watching how much I spent.

The following afternoon, I went to the interview that was held on the first floor of the County administrative building in the Human Resources Department. I entered a room, and I found many interview candidates waiting. The interview was short, less than fifteen minutes, and I was asked about my education and prior experience. I was informed that those advancing in the process would be called back for a second interview.

I spent a second night in Riverside and flew back to Seattle the next day, not having any conviction that I had performed well enough to be called back. Prior experience had taught me not to hold my hopes high and instead to wait to hear from the employers. I knew the interview was short and easy, but still, I did not hold my hopes too high.

On a Wednesday, three weeks after I interviewed, I went to work as on any normal day. When I returned home, I found a piece of mail with a return address for the County of Riverside. I tore it open along the perforated edge to read it. It was a congratulatory letter that I had successfully completed the first phase of the interview and that I was being invited to attend the second part, this time with the hiring department. Like the first invitation letter, I was asked to call within three days to confirm that I would attend. I confirmed my attendance. I then started looking for money to buy an airline ticket to fly back to Southern California one other time. My friends thought I was going nuts flying to California again for an interview. I had been to two interviews already and had no job offer. I paid no attention to them, and I continued my preparations to travel. My gut feeling was that this time, I had a good chance of getting the job.

I made arrangements at my job to take time off so that I could attend the interview. I was an intern, and I thought that asking for time off yet again would likely not reflect well on my work ethic. I asked for time off anyway. I recall my supervisor commenting that she understood my situation since the internship was only temporary, with a possibility that the city council would not fund the position past the allocated time. Her comments made me believe that she knew that I was looking for a permanent job. I had not given her the reason why I needed the time off, but she had guessed right.

I flew into Ontario airport again and rode a bus to Riverside. This time, the interview questions were about planning, reading architectural and grading plans, and suggesting development solutions for a site with drainage issues. I read and interpreted the architectural and engineering drawings with ease. I made suggestions as to what the best way would be to develop the sites. Reading architectural and engineering drawings posed no difficulty to me, for I had by then spent time drawing plans and reading drawings. I had spent countless hours in design studios in college and spent months working for the City of Seattle, producing drawings. The interview lasted about thirty minutes, and it was a breeze. I felt very confident that I had performed well.

The next day, I flew back to Seattle and was ready to go back to my job at the City of Tukwila. They already had suspicions that I was searching for a job, but they did not ask me to tell them where I was on those days I was off. In the days that followed, the head of the Department approached me and offered to extend my time at Tukwila. He told me that the Department had a new project that had been authorized by the City Council and that they would like me to take on that project. It was still going to be a temporary position and would have required council approval for extensions. He also told me that there was a strong possibility that a new position could be created in the department. But all that would have been dependent on money being allocated in the following year's budget. I had a feeling that they liked the work I was doing.

To me, the job I was doing was temporary, and it had been approaching two years since I graduated. I had not landed the permanent job I desired. I had put my foot in the door, I had built up experience, and I wanted to start building a career. I told the head of the Department that I would be interested in extending my internship. I informed him that my priority was having a permanent job that offered me benefits, such as retirement and health insurance.

One afternoon, while I was working at my desk, which was just outside of my supervisor's office, a phone call came in from my boss. The caller asked my supervisor by name, and she confirmed that it was her on the phone. At first, I could overhear much of what she was saying on the phone. Then she started talking in a low voice, so I could hardly hear her. With the few words I could hear, I got a strong suspicion that the phone call was about me and that someone was calling to check my references. After the call ended, she walked away from her office without saying a word to me.

At the end of the day, I went home; I did not talk to my boss for the rest of the day. When I got home, I saw a blinking light on my phone, indicating that there was a message waiting to be retrieved. The message was for me to call the County of Riverside about a job opening and the interview I had attended. I put the pieces of the puzzle together, overhearing my boss's phone conversation and the phone message, and right there and then, I knew that the news from my interview was positive. It was in the evening after office hours in California, so I could not call back to Riverside County. It was a good, positive feeling, though, that I had that whole night.

The following morning, I wrote down the phone number displayed on the phone caller identification, and I took it with me to work. During my lunch break, I drove to Tukwila Mall, found a call box, and made a phone call to the Riverside County planning department. A gentleman answered the call, and I told him who I was and why I was calling. He told me that he was offering a planning position with the County of Riverside and wanted to know if I was still interested in the position. Without any hesitation, I gladly answered yes, that I was still interested in the job. He asked me when I would like to start. I was going to give my employer two weeks' notice, and I would need a week to prepare for my move to California. So, I told him my start date would be three weeks away, at the end of September 1987.

On September 28, at eight o'clock in the morning, I reported for work on the ninth floor of the County administrative building. I had finally landed a permanent job with full benefits, and I was ready to uproot myself from Washington State to California.

The people I worked with at the City of Tukwila were quite nice throughout my stay. They were willing to help me with information any time I ran into a problem. I felt obligated to return the favor. Although I was a temporary employee and did not have to give them notice that I was leaving the job, I gave them two weeks' notice, and I informed them that I was moving to California to start a new job with the Riverside County Planning Department. They expressed to me how sad they were that I was leaving. The head of the department commented that he had been working to find more work for me if I wanted to change my mind and stay with the Tukwila Planning Department.

Tukwila was a good place to work, but the major concern to me was that the job was temporary. Its continued existence was dependent on the City Council approving the funding. Riverside County was offering me a full-time, permanent position with full benefits. I was going to be getting paid vacation, paid sick leave, and a guaranteed retirement. Furthermore, the jobs recession within the Seattle metro area was not easing up. Considering all those factors I did not see a bright future staying with the City of Tukwila.

In the afternoon, on my last day of work, the staff in the Planning Department took me out for a farewell lunch and wished me well. We talked about how I was going to handle the relocation, and I told them a little bit about my relocation plans. I was going to drive to California by myself, find an apartment, and then drive back to Seattle and pick up my family and personal belongings. They offered a few suggestions on driving long distances, the dos and don'ts of long-distance driving, and what safety issues I needed to observe. The lunch conversation was friendly, and at the end of the day, I said goodbye to all, and I left the City of Tukwila employment.

## How The Move Affected Mary: The Dilemma

After the farewell and resignation, there was no turning back. I had no job in Washington State and all my future was in California. When I got home, I started putting together plans to relocate. I started packing my belongings and prepared to travel to California alone, leaving my family behind. I had to be in California to look for an apartment before I brought the children to Riverside.

A year and a half prior, my sister Mary had arrived from Uganda to attend school at Shoreline Community College in Seattle. She was new to the country and was adjusting to the new environment and social settings. She had come on a student visa, which required her to stay enrolled in school. There was the question of how to relocate her without missing out on her school and violating her student visa. I had no answer to that question as I started preparing to move to California. I could not find permanent work in Seattle, and I had to relocate.

I had decided that taking a job in California was the right decision since I finally had a great opportunity to start my planning career. Not taking that job and staying in Seattle, where there were no jobs, would have been a big mistake. We decided that to continue attending school and not violate her student visa, my sister had to stay in Seattle for one school quarter. During that time, she would apply to Riverside Community College (RCC) for a transfer. That way, her visa would have remained valid. Once admitted to RCC, she would come and join me and the rest of the family in California. I talked to friends in Seattle and asked them if they would share living arrangements with my sister during that application period. Arrangements were made for her to temporarily stay with a friend with whom she shared an apartment.

Those were hard times financially. My pay at my new job with Riverside County could not go very far, considering that I had two children to care for and whose mother did not have a job. I had to pay rent for the apartment we lived in. I also had a couple of car payments to make. Added to those responsibilities was one of supporting my sister I left behind in Seattle. I had to find money to pay her tuition at the community college in Seattle and money to cover her day-to-day expenses. There were times when I would question myself if I had made the right decision to relocate. But then I would quickly tell myself that nothing good in this world is earned easily or delivered on a silver platter. Hence, I decided to continue pushing to pay for everything that had to be paid for.

The car payments were a burden; however, stopping making them up was not an option. We moved to Southern California, where it is almost impossible to do daily functions without a car. It was common for employers to ask if one had a car during the interview before they were offered a job. Little could be done without a car, especially since we were moving to a city with minimal public transportation.

My sister would call me asking for financial help, and I would help her as much as I could. When I did not have the money to send her, my friend in Seattle, whom I went to school with, stepped in. He offered to lend me money so that Mary could continue to go to school and buy necessities. We agreed on the loan arrangements, and he gave her the money. I paid him back fully in monthly installments. In the meantime, I was pushing my sister to complete her application so she could transfer to Riverside Community College (RCC). She decided not to send the application to RCC, and she did not relocate to California. As time went by, she was able to establish herself financially by finding a job. By that time, the whole idea of her moving to California was dead.

Helping my relatives, I left home in Uganda was an idea that never died. I had it on my mind as I flew to the United States in 1982, and I still held on to that idea until 1988. I had worked at Riverside County for a year, and I started to work to help my niece to apply to Riverside Community College. She applied and was admitted, and I made her travel arrangements to travel to California from Uganda. She came over and started going to school, sharing living arrangements with me.

Soon, there were conflicts between my niece and Jayke, who threatened to move out of the apartment with the children if I did not evict my niece. She wanted to move out and file for child support. She had no job at the time. That put me in a dilemma. My niece was new in the country, and I had signed her sponsorship forms to get a student visa to study at RCC. I could not tell her to move out of the apartment, she had no income, and she was my responsibility financially. She was going to school as a full-time student and with no work authorization from the Immigration and Naturalization Service (INS). The agency has since been renamed and split into three departments: US Citizenship and Immigration Services (USCIS), US Immigration and Customs Enforcement (ICE), and US Customs and Border Protection (CBP).

One evening, I came home from work and found Jayke had put the children in the car and driven off to Texas. I did not hear from her for two days until she got to Dallas. When she called, she told me that if I did not get my niece out of the apartment, she was not going to come back to Riverside and that she had already put in an application for child support in Texas.

I had to find a solution to the problem that had cropped up. I could not afford to pay child support for three children and pay for my living expenses in California. I discussed the issue with my sister in Seattle to come up with a solution. We decided that my niece would move to Seattle to live with her. She was on a student visa, and for her to live in Seattle, she had to transfer to Shoreline Community College. That is what she did, and at the end of the school year, she moved to Seattle. She successfully transferred to Shoreline Community College, and after she had moved out of the apartment, Jayke returned to Riverside with the children.

The financial arrangements were still tight. Thankfully, she finished her education, and now she is well-established in the nursing profession. The important lesson to learn from all this is that without pain, there are no good things in life you can get. The whole idea is to persevere and not ever lose hope, knowing that nothing is unachievable.

Years passed, and I got a request from my older brother in Uganda, who had children but had limited means of putting them through school. One of his sons was ready to attend college; however, my brother had no financial means of sending him to college. He asked if I could help with financial assistance. I was fortunate that I had the financial means to assist by that time. I sent him to Ukraine to attend medical school. After he finished medical school, he came to the United States, where he is now employed.

# Chapter 9
## The Move To California

In 1985, I graduated with a master's degree from the University of Washington School of Architecture and Urban Planning, a college-wide urban design program. I acquired planning, architectural, and landscape architectural skills. By the time 1987 came around, I had applied those skills at the City of Seattle and the City of Tukwila. I had landed a job in California; I was feeling good about myself.

When I told friends that I was moving to California for a job, some did not think it was a good idea, while others thought I should chase my dreams. Those friends who knew of my immigration status were concerned that I did not have permanent immigration authorization to work in the US. By then, I was being granted work authorization that lasted six months and had to be renewed every so often. My friends were concerned that I would be stuck in California without a job if the immigration authorities did not renew my work authorization. That did not faze me at all; I packed my belongings, put them in a small Toyota Corolla, and drove to California.

I had never driven such an interstate long distance. I was going to drive over 1,200 miles for at least 18 hours driving from Seattle to Riverside. I left Seattle at midnight and drove south on Interstate Highway Five, stopping at rest places for about 30 minutes to stretch, walk around, and use restrooms. At a couple of rest stops, I spent hours sleeping in my Toyota car. The money was tight, and I could not afford to pay for a hotel. I needed every penny I had to take me through to my first paycheck at my new job working at the County of Riverside. I was able to handle the long drive, for I was in my youthful years; my body could easily handle the drive.

Before starting my journey, I went to a local American Automobile Association (AAA) office in Seattle to get maps with directions that I used to drive the 1,200 miles to Riverside. Back in 1987, there was no internet, let alone digital maps. Travelers used paper maps for road directions. AAA gave me road maps from Seattle to Riverside covering the states of Washington, Oregon, and California. Driving was relatively easy since I followed Interstate Highway 5 up to Los Angeles. When I reached Los Angeles, I relied on AAA maps to get me to Riverside.

I arrived in Riverside at night, and I decided that it was not a good idea to pay for a motel room where I was going to sleep for just a few hours. I inquired at one of the motels along University Avenue about the cost of a room. I confirmed my suspicion about the cost of the rooms and felt very good about my decision not to get a room.

After inquiring, I asked the person at the counter if I could park in the motel parking lot for the rest of the night. He agreed to let me park overnight. Having been so tired from driving for over 18 hours, as soon as I parked the vehicle and reclined the front seat on the driver's side, I fell asleep. I did not wake up until daylight the following morning.

The challenge in the morning was to find a place to wash my face, brush my teeth, and freshen up. I found a McDonald's restaurant where I bought breakfast, washed my face, brushed my teeth, and changed clothes. I spent the following day looking for a motel where I could stay while I looked for an apartment. Once I found one, I checked in, made myself comfortable, and rested.

The next day, I reported to the county offices for my new job. I was to report to the Planning Department at eight in the morning. I showed up ready for work but was very worried about my immigration work authorization. I knew I had to show and prove my legal authorization to work. By the time I left Seattle, my work authorization papers were coming up for renewal. The lady in the planning department asked me to present papers that allowed me to work. I took out documents that were listed as acceptable for verification of work authorization.

She accepted the documents and took photocopies, and I was officially a County of Riverside employee. Had my papers been rejected by the county, I would have been in a disastrous situation. I would have had to decide whether to drive back to Seattle or stay in California and look for another job where my papers would be accepted. Relocation to California was a big risk I took and that could have resulted in major negative ramifications had I not been successful. But again, if you don't take risks, you never get anything accomplished.

By having my work authorization papers accepted, I had jumped one major hurdle. My next task was to look for an apartment around town where I could make my new home in

California. Having lived in Seattle's University District for most of my stay in Seattle, I was drawn to look at rentals around the University of California Riverside (UCR) campus. I wanted an area that had people from many different countries, and which had places where I could go and expand my knowledge. UCR had a library, a diverse student population by country of origin, and was close to my work.

I got a two-bedroom apartment along Iowa Avenue. To get the apartment, I was asked to prove that I had employment and show my pay stubs. I didn't have any paystubs from my new job since I was new and was not paid yet. In addition, I did not have the first and last month's rent money. I had to come up with a solution. I negotiated with the manager of the apartment complex. I explained to her that I was new in the area and had just started a new job at the County of Riverside. At first, she didn't seem to believe me. She decided to investigate, and she asked for the name of my supervisor at the county. I gave her the name, and she told me to come back the following day to know the decision about my application. She called the county and spoke to my supervisor.

When I returned the following day, she had decided to give me the apartment. Now we had to negotiate how to handle payment of the first and last month's money. I told her that I would pay half of the current month's rent, and when I got my first check, I would pay the remainder of the rent and half of the last month. We agreed that in two months I would be caught up with my payments with the deposit paid and the rent brought current. I lived up to my promise and made all the payments on time.

I had an apartment, so my next move was to go back to Seattle and bring my family down to California. That took a lot of planning since I had no vacation time at my new job, and I couldn't ask for days off from work where I had barely worked for two weeks. Luckily, there was a Columbus Day public holiday that fell on the second Monday of October. That gave me a three-day weekend, the time I was not required to be at work, and enough time to plan my move to Seattle and back to Riverside.

On a Friday after work, I went home, had dinner, had a nap, and at midnight, I got into my Toyota Corolla and started driving up north on Interstate Highway 5 to Seattle. This time, I had experience driving long distances, and the journey was not as taxing as the first time I drove it. As before, I did not spend a night in motel rooms. I got to Seattle on a Saturday evening, and as I had instructed, the family was ready for the move. After separating the children's belongings, the rest of the stuff, like the large items and not-so-essential items, were shipped by a moving company from Seattle to Riverside. I found the moving company while I was in Riverside, and movers picked up the items before I got to Seattle.

There were two vehicles to be driven from Seattle to Riverside. I put personal belongings in the two vehicles. On Sunday afternoon, I had everyone in the cars, and we started driving down to California. This time, since I had children, I planned on spending a night in a hotel. I needed to rest and sleep for at least 8 hours. The safety of the children was very important. We spent Sunday night in a hotel, and the following morning, we started driving down to California, arriving in the city of Riverside at night on Monday. On Tuesday morning, I was at my job, having completed moving the family to California in an environment that was new to everybody.

I worked with the County of Riverside from September 1987 to January 1989. During that time, the county was undergoing a major transformation from a rural agricultural county to a modern suburban metro area. Many people were moving from the Los Angeles, Orange, and San Diego Counties into Riverside in what was known as the "Move East" phenomenon. Hundreds of thousands of people migrated inland to take advantage of cheaper, newer housing. Citrus farms that covered large stretches of Riverside County were being cleared to allow for the building of new homes, shopping centers, warehouses, restaurants, apartments, and schools. My first job assignment was to change the County's General Plan. It was the county's central policy document, and I had to amend it to get rid of policies that required lands to be used for citrus farms and allow for the development of urban projects.

Those actions allowed rural agricultural areas to develop into the modern cities of Murrieta, Temecula, Moreno Valley, and several other present-day cities. I have fresh memories of projects that I worked on and watched their transformation into urban areas. I would drive south to vineyards and citrus farms in Murrieta and Temecula areas that are now shopping malls, homes, casinos, and hospitals. Meetings with landowners, developers, civil engineers, architects, and contractors were constantly ongoing.

In as much as the job was interesting because I had to drive to many areas of the county, it posed a problem when I had to travel to the neighboring San Diego County border. Just south of Temecula, there was an immigration checkpoint. Vehicles had to stop at the checkpoint to be inspected by immigration officers looking for people without a legal right to be in the US. On a Wednesday afternoon, I traveled south on Interstate Highway 15 toward the San Diego border with a county colleague. She drove south on Interstate Highway 15 past Temecula and the immigration inspection point. After passing the checkpoint, the staff exited and started driving back north on the interstate highway toward the inspection checkpoint. When we arrived at the checkpoint, we stopped, and the immigration officer asked where we were going. We replied that we were Riverside County employees who were in the area doing county work. The immigration personnel let us continue without looking at our immigration papers or driver's licenses.

At that time, I had legal permission to stay in the United States under a special program that allowed Ugandans to live in the US. I could exit the country but could not freely re-enter. With my immigration status being unclear I got worried that I would be removed from the county vehicle and asked to explain my immigration status. Luckily, we went through the checkpoint without incident. I returned to Riverside without being questioned. Up to now, I wonder what my co-worker intended by driving me through the immigration checkpoint. Had she suspected that I did not have proper immigration papers and wanted me deported? Or did she want to intimidate me so that I would pay special respect to her? Did I pose a threat of some sort to her at work? Did she feel like I would take her job? But for sure, the moment when I realized that we were driving through an immigration checkpoint was very terrifying. I started thinking of what would happen to my two little kids; where would they have lived if I had been detained?

# Chapter 10
## Joining The City Of Riverside

After a year and a half with Riverside County, I applied for a job at the City of Riverside. The city was looking to fill a position that focused on architectural and grading plan reviews for proposed development projects. The city was growing rapidly and wanted to ensure that the projects constructed were of high design standards.

I was invited for an interview scheduled for 10 a.m. I left the job at the county during my morning break and walked a couple of blocks to the city hall building for the interview. I did not request time off work because the meeting was scheduled to last thirty minutes. We took breaks that lasted thirty minutes at the county, so I figured I could fit the interview during the break time. At worst, I could stretch my break by fifteen minutes without major consequences.

The interviewers were interested in knowing more about my architectural skills and how they could be applied to the position. They wanted to make sure that I would fit into the design review section and that I would hit the ground running because there were many development plans awaiting review. Already, there was someone in the section who was good at landscape architecture. The head of the section was strong in architecture but could not work on all the plans that were submitted. I answered all the interview questions with ease, and in the end, I felt very confident that I convinced them I possessed the skills for the job.

A few days later, I received a phone call inviting me to return for a second interview, this time with the planning director and his deputy. I was informed that the interview would last no more than thirty minutes, and I was urged to arrive on time. At ten o'clock, I was at the planning department office, and the interview started on time.

The questions were not challenging. The interviewers asked if I was to stay in the USA for a long time and if I had any familial ties to the area and the country. I informed them that I have children born in this country. I had decided to raise the kids in this country to avail them of more life opportunities. I also said that I have other relatives in the country.

Seven days later, the planning deputy director called to offer me the job. I accepted the offer and put in my two-week notice to resign from the county. My coworkers asked me how and when I interviewed for the job. I disclosed to them that I took trips to city hall to interview during my breaks. On my last day, my workmates took me out to lunch.

On a morning in January 1989, I reported for work at Riverside City Hall. As was routine and required by the law, I was asked to show my work authorization documents before starting work, which I did. During the Christmas week of 1988, I went to the Immigration and Naturalization Office in River side and applied to get a green card. My application was accepted, and I was permitted to work. The document was to expire in three months, after which time I would go back and renew it.

Before reporting for work, the city had sent me to a laboratory to give blood and a urine sample for drug screening. The day I reported for work, the results were not yet back from the lab. I went to the third floor without going to the Human Resources Department. Three days later, I was approached by one of the supervisors who told me to go to human resources. My heart was pounding, thinking that I was being called in because of my work authorization documents. I knew, however, that I could work legally, and my only worry at the time was whether the permit would be renewed after three months.

A person at the human resources office told me that my lab results had come back inconclusive. He told me to leave the job and only return after I received a call from the department. After two days, I called the human resources department to find out what was going on. They told me they asked for a re-test of the samples and did not have the results from the lab. I drove to the lab to enquire, and the lab technician told me that they had found a substance in the results that I had not listed on the form I filled out which asked to list all medications taken in the previous two weeks. I didn't list any medication since I knew that I took no medications in the specified time. The lab results showed ingredients for Nyquil, an over-the-counter cold medication and one prescription medicine.

I went back to city hall and spoke to Human Resources, and I told them what I found out from the laboratory. The human resources staff said the Nyquil was not listed but was not of concern to them since it was readily available over the counter. The staff mentioned a prescription medication that I had not listed on the intake form. She asked me to prove that

I had a prescription from a doctor for that medication. I went back to my apartment and picked up the bottle, which had the doctor's name and displayed the name of the medication. After looking at the label, the staff made photocopies. She told me to wait in the lobby as she made phone calls and later told me to leave. The following day, my supervisor called me to report for work again at city hall. If I had not taken the initiative to go back to the lab to inquire as to what was really going on with my drug test results, I could have ended up without a job.

## My Experience Working At The City Of Riverside

As stated above, I started work at the Riverside County Planning Department in September 1987. Within one year, I worked on diverse project proposals that came into the county for review and issuance of development permits. The county was transforming from a predominantly rural agricultural area into several modern suburban neighborhoods with new shopping malls, apartments, single-family residences, offices, and commercial strip malls.

At that time, huge chunks of land comprising thousands and thousands of acres were under agricultural preserves. California State regulations restricted removing land from the agricultural preserve category to urban uses. Agriculture plays a major role in the state's economy, and there was a desire to preserve the sector. Citrus farms, vegetable farms, and ranches that stretched for miles produced a variety of agricultural produce. The owners of the farms and ranches, especially those along major highways and with proximity to big urban areas, started applying to the state to take their land out of the agricultural preserves. Taking them out of the agricultural preserve status meant that those lands could be developed with urban uses such as shopping malls, dense housing, single-family residences and so forth. The owners had calculated that they could get a lot more money by pulling the farms and ranches out of agricultural preserve status and putting them under more intensive urban land use.

That was the time when a population shift in the area was taking place. People were moving out of the more crowded and more expensive areas of Los Angeles, Orange County, and San Diego into the less populated areas in Riverside County. The areas surrounding the City of Riverside and extending all the way to the San Diego County border along the highways were aggressively being pulled out of agricultural preserve status. Riverside County was responsible for development controls in those areas since they were not incorporated as cities. Areas currently occupied by the City of Moreno Valley, Perris, Temecula, Murrieta, Eastvale, Jurupa Valley, Menifee, and the City of Hemet were all under the County jurisdiction for planning and development purposes.

Every time I go to those malls or drive through those cities, my mind goes back to the late 1980s and 1990s, and I remember the work I did. I feel proud that, in some way, I contributed to the development of those areas that have now become successful commercial, industrial, or office areas. Every development brings back memories of what it was like working on those developments.

It was in January 1989 that I made a career move, leaving the County of Riverside and joining the City of Riverside just a couple of blocks away. Prior to that date, I had applied for a job with the city in 1987 while still in Seattle, Washington, but never made it to the interview. I was excited to be joining the city.

Above, I talked about the interview process and how the city staff wanted to know if I had the design skills to do the job. It was perfect work for me because my new duties were to be in planning, urban design and architecture, where I had the most experience and had acquired great skills while in college.

Having been assigned to the planning department's design review section, I reviewed architectural and engineering drawings for proposed development projects. The work was different from the duties I had at the county, where I worked on projects that were still in their infancy and in areas still under agriculture. The projects in the city were more detailed and in the final stages of the development review and permitting process, just before the buildings were constructed and occupied. I was a contact person for the projects through the review and construction period. I frequently visited construction sites, and I was involved in the final inspections and issuance of the occupancy permits once the construction was completed.

Working on those projects exposed me to people in different areas of design, construction, and, most importantly, to people who invested in real estate. I worked with developers, financiers, builders, and people who sold real estate. That exposure would end up having a profound influence on me, and it played a big part in what made me focus even more on investing in real estate. I admired how those people who came in and whose projects I worked on were able to put together a team to design, construct, advertise, and sell the buildings that I reviewed at work. I would imagine myself being in their position, owning buildings and arranging financing for the developments. Getting into real estate investing became a top priority on the list of things I had to accomplish.

Like the County areas, the City of Riverside was going through a time of rapid development and transformation. There were big residential, commercial, and industrial developments under construction, and existing shopping malls were under rapid expansion. Areas that had been under orange groves were being developed with shopping centers, office complexes, and industrial buildings at a rapid pace. With that growth, there was plenty of work to be done at City Hall. To stay current with the workload, I would take work home to work over the weekend. Every two weeks on Wednesday, the Design Review Board held public meetings to review development plans. The reports and project plans that were to be reviewed at the meetings were to be ready on Monday. Working over the weekend allowed me to have the reports and plans ready on Monday.

It was a hectic time at the city offices, and some of the people who were hired at the same time as I was resigned and went on to other jobs, citing the heavy workload involved. Thanks to my background in design, I could review those drawings with ease, and I was able to stay on top of my assignments.

In the first three years after I joined the city, the work environment was cordial, with members of the Planning Department working well together. Promotional opportunities came up, and competition for those jobs started to cause cracks in the friendly work relationships. People started seeing each other as competitors and a threat to their career advancements.

As is often the case in such workplace competitions, racial, ethnic, and national divisions emerged. Some people resented being supervised by people of certain races or nationalities. Others thought that if a black person were made a supervisor, they would treat them unfairly. They thought that there would be some form of revenge. My counterargument to those kinds of arguments was that if you don't want to live in that kind of fear, the fear of revenge, then don't engage in any actions that may cause divisions.

The Planning Department did not have black senior management staff to act as a role model for other black employees. I worked at the city for over 25 years, and the Planning Department never had a black person in a top senior management position, even though many highly qualified black individuals worked in the department. When it came to making career opportunities available to black employees, the County performed far better than the city. When I worked for the county, there were several black senior staff members. The City Planning Department had no role models for black employees to look up to or to emulate to get into those roles. On the other hand, there was always no shortage of role models for white employees, and their careers rapidly advanced. When asked why there were no black senior staff, I was told that they could not find qualified candidates. I found that argument to lack any merits. The department promoted people of other races who had less experience and education and had not worked on or accomplished major assignments in the department. Those employees were promoted and bypassed black candidates with greater experience and education.

I constantly improved my job skills by attending conferences and seminars. I was a member of the American Planning Association, the American Institute of Certified Planners, and an Associate member of the American Institute of Architects. Except for the head of the department, I became the only member of the AICP in the department at the time. When I took the exams and became a member of the American Institute of Certified Planners, the intent was to improve my chances of advancement in the planning profession.

While I was only the second person to be a member of the AICP in the department, my chances of career advancement never improved. Before I passed the exams, being an AICP was always being praised as a great achievement. It was treasured in the department as a great step toward career advancement. When it came to me, the membership did not mean anything; it was discounted to the level of being nothing.

Not long after I passed the AICP examinations, a promotional position opened in the department. The job announcement was written in such a way that it intentionally mentioned that the AICP membership was an added advantage. I was the only candidate interviewed with the membership. Despite all my qualifications matching the position, I did not get the promotion, instead, it went to someone of lesser qualifications and shorter experience.

A year went by, and another promotional position opened up, and a job announcement was posted. By then, another black employee had passed the AICP examinations. Again, the announcement specified that having an AICP was an added advantage. I applied for the position, and again, neither I nor the other black employee who was an AICP member got the promotion. Instead, the position was offered to a person who had just received the AICP certification but with less experience.

In a congratulatory message that was sent out to the department, the head of the department specifically mentioned that that person was promoted because of her accomplishment of passing the AICP examinations. I felt there was unfairness. When I was the only candidate with the AICP certification, it did not carry any weight at all. After some other person of a different race got the certification, it weighed heavily in the decision toward the promotion. It was a double standard; black people were judged using a different standard. Different reasons were given for not promoting a black person, and those reasons directly conflicted with each other.

My frustrations mounted; it was unfair to promote people with less experience and less education. I felt there was racial discrimination happening, and I needed to confront the situation. I filed a complaint with the Human Resources

Department. I was not satisfied with the results of their investigation, so I filed a complaint with the Equal Employment Opportunity Commission (EEOC).

My experience filing such discrimination complaints was that it is close to impossible to get a positive result. A black attorney told me that anti-discrimination laws exist on the books. They don't offer much protection to black people against discrimination. The laws have gaping holes for the employers to find a way to circumvent them.

As is common practice, the violators blame the victims and smear them with negative propaganda. I was attacked from all corners by the same people who denied me a promotion, accusing me of all sorts of negative things. It was their way of justifying their actions. In frustration, my other black colleague with AICP certification quit the job.

In 2002, my frustration peaked after I had heard all sorts of excuses as to why I was not being promoted and being negatively attacked. By then, I had gained much experience and worked on all types of projects that the planning department reviews. In the interviews, I would point out my strengths and the fact that I have worked on all types of projects in the department. It never mattered. A new person would be hired or promoted, and I would be assigned to work with that individual to train them. The reason given for the assignment was that I had a thorough knowledge of the entire department and how it functions. I was, therefore, the perfect person to train or give guidance to those newly hired or promoted employees. It allowed the individuals to get their footing and learn their new duties. There were times when employees would be hired, and after I trained them and had gained knowledge of the job and functioning of the department, they would be given more attractive assignments, and they would be promoted to supervise me.

On one occasion, a top management person with little knowledge about planning was assigned to oversee planning functions, a field she did not know much about. She did not know much about planning, so she was made my supervisor so that I could train her in planning functions. I would review development projects and write a report with my name as the author; however, by the time the report was published, my name would be removed and another person inserted as the author.

Those kinds of actions and the discrimination in the promotion process forced me to spend more time looking for ideas where I controlled the outcome. I did not want to be doing the work and someone else taking the credit. I wanted to be doing things the results of which gave me feel a sense of accomplishment.

I read books about self-improvement and about people who worked on their own and got big accomplishments. When I started my planning career, I had a desire to climb up the bureaucratic ladder and be one of the top individuals in the establishment. I had worked for years, and I was not feeling a sense of accomplishment. By 2002, I had adjusted my thinking on what I wanted to do to have a sense of accomplishment. I had come to realize that advancing to the top of an organization in the USA, where I was an immigrant and a black person, was not going to happen.

I had also concluded that reaching the top of the organization would only bring me psychological fulfillment. It was not going to give me financial independence. The personal sacrifices that would lead to reaching the top of the organization did not match the financial benefits. There was so much to overcome as a black, foreign-born individual.

I then looked at the people who had climbed up the hierarchy and had top positions in the organization. These were people I initially admired and looked at as my role models. I became less impressed by what they considered to be their big accomplishments. I did not see much that was required to demonstrate individual innovative ideas. I looked at them as filling positions with established organizational structures that limited individual innovation. They filled positions that already existed with established standard operating procedures, and all that was to be done to be successful was to implement those procedures. There was little or no innovation needed to be considered successful in the position.

What I considered success and accomplishment was going out there, coming up with original ideas, and building a system or business from scratch. One had to come up with innovative ideas and implement them without being tied down by the limitations of the organization. I considered that to be different from filling a job position only to implement rules and policies set by the organization.

With those new convictions and having a different perspective of what it meant to be successful and accomplished, combined with the discrimination I encountered, I focused on starting and doing my own business and investments. What my parents told me when I was little was in play. Someone chasing you gives you clues as to what you need to do to escape. This time, my drive to do my own ventures was a result of the discriminators' actions.

I read several books about people who started individual businesses. The authors expressed a feeling of accomplishment. People talked about coming up with an idea and nurturing it to maturity like they were nurturing a child. They talked about eventually being rewarded handsomely financially. Those books pointed out that most wealthy people become millionaires by coming up with ideas that they develop into money-making ventures. They put in individual effort and reaped huge rewards. They worked long hours every day, knowing that the rewards to be had were not going to end up with some other person.

# Chapter 11

## My Experiences As A Family Man

It was in 1982 that I started attending classes at the University of Washington. When I started the classes, most of my time was devoted to studying, and I rarely traveled off campus. I did not meet other Ugandans or Africans who did not attend classes on campus. It wasn't until I was in my second year of school that I met a Ugandan who was working at Radio Shack on University Avenue in the University District. I was looking to buy an entertainment system for my room. I entered the store, and he approached me.

"How can I help?" he asked me.

"I am looking for a stereo system," I replied.

"Look at this one. It is new on the market," he said.

"Can I listen to it?" I asked.

Before he started playing a song on the stereo, he asked me, "Are you from Africa?" I replied yes. He then asked which country I was from, and I replied that I was from Uganda.

"So am I," he said. There and then, we started conversing in our native dialect Luganda. He continued to do a demonstration on the stereo.

He then said, "This stereo is 900 dollars."

"That is very expensive. I can't afford it," I told him.

"If you like, I can sell you a used one that I own," he said.

I needed a stereo system for my room to keep my mind off the books I used to study the entire day, and I was looking to listen to music as a form of relaxation.

"I would like to see your stereo system," I told him.

"Okay. Come back later tonight when I am off work, and I will take you to see it," he said.

"That's all right," I told him.

In the evening, I met him at the store, and we walked to his apartment. After I listened to his stereo system, I was impressed, and we negotiated a price. We settled on $350, and I bought it that night. He helped me transport it to my room. Before we parted, he gave me his phone number and suggested that we should meet for dinner.

After a few weeks, he organized a dinner party at his house and invited his coworker and two brothers from Uganda who shared an apartment in the adjacent neighborhood. The younger of the two brothers was attending a University in Seattle downtown. During my short two-week school break, I went to their apartment to watch Sunday football. During our conversation, they mentioned that there were other Ugandans whom they often hang out with. It was yet another chance to get to know more people. The brothers had stories about two women who they said were friends with and lived in an apartment building close by.

On a Halloween day, I got a call from Jayke, one of those women who introduced herself to me over the phone. She said that she wanted to meet me and suggested that she was going to be in the University District where I lived. She wanted to stop by my apartment, and I gave her my address. She showed up mid-morning with a painted face. She was going to attend a Halloween party. She asked if I wanted to accompany her to the party, and I accepted. We drove to a house where a group of people had gathered to enjoy treats and Halloween games. The host asked if I wanted to play the games, and I agreed to join in playing the games. It was my first Halloween in the United States, and many of the games were new to me. I also did not know much about Halloween, and I got to ask questions to learn more. That is a day that was not celebrated in Uganda.

We stayed at the party for a couple of hours, then drove back to the University District, where I was dropped off at my apartment. We kept communicating by phone for a while and went to the movies a couple of times. We got to know each other, and our friendship grew stronger, and we started dating. Our relationship became serious, and after some time, we had a son born in 1984. After a couple of years, we had a second child, a girl.

The longer we stayed together, the more Jayke was expressing to me that she made a big mistake being in our relationship. She was concerned that her parents would not approve of the relationship, and I could not understand why a grown woman like her needed the approval of her parents to be in a relationship. Soon, I had serious concerns that I was with a person who could not make her own decisions but rather relied on others to make major decisions in her life. Approval from her parents was more important to her than raising her children to have a good future.

For me, I believed that the decision between two people to be in a relationship was theirs. I told her that I wanted us to decide our destiny and not the other individuals she wanted to introduce into our relationship. I did not see relatives' approval as paramount for us to work together. I viewed relatives as advisers who would be consulted if needed but not to seek approval for a personal decision to be in a relationship. The same goes for a person's color, ethnic background, or country of origin. I believe that every individual makes his or her decision as to whom to associate with. I was brought up to treat people the same regardless of where they are from or their ethnicity. I consider a successful relationship to be based on how the two people align their beliefs on important aspects of life. Jayke's beliefs were different from mine in this area. She believed that a person's start in life outweighed anything else an individual had accomplished in life. I held out hope that she would change her views and judge people based on their accomplishments.

She believed that a person's worth in society or life achievement is determined by the accident of their birth and not their efforts in life. According to her beliefs, a person's status is determined at birth regardless of their accomplishments. I believe that a person's status in society depends on what the individual accomplishes. Anyone can achieve whatever they set out to do, with their place of birth playing an insignificant role.

I do not put what anyone's parents achieved ahead of one's effort and accomplishments. I believed in that principle when I was younger, and I still do to this day. In fact, when I look back over the years, I realize that there are many people I have known who put their parents' achievements on top of their individual accomplishments or as the only thing that made them feel worthwhile. Those individuals did not achieve much in life. While the past should not be forgotten, it should not be the primary factor in making life decisions or forging relationships in our lives.

Several people who come to America from other countries, including African countries, tend to bring with them norms from their countries. The United States has different norms and societal perceptions of being accomplished. People fail to adjust their thinking to realize that whatever the family status was back home before they came to the USA, personal effort, accomplishments, and self-improvement are what is vital. This country is the "equalizer." It does not matter what kind of life you lived before you came here; you have to work to uplift yourself. Jayke seemed to hold on to childhood customs when she felt that she had to get approval from her parents. Educational achievement, a good job, and individual financial achievements were irrelevant to her.

Likewise, some individuals refuse to take starter jobs because they consider their parents were so highly placed in their native country. A starter job, no matter how small it is, helps to get your foot in the door of the American workplace. Such a job leads to better work and a better life. Being in a new country, one has to be hungry when it comes to searching for financial success. Sticking to the past becomes an obstacle to advancement. Telling someone in this country that I used to live in a posh neighborhood before I immigrated or that I went to the best school in my native country is a waste of time. It would make no sense to that individual because, in this country, personal effort and accomplishment are what matters most.

Because my vision of life was very different from Jayke's, we became ideologically detached with a different outlook on life, and I did not feel that I had a partner in life. I started to feel doubtful that I could convince her to look at life differently and not through her parents' life. Life is what you make of it. Challenging oneself to achieve more than what your parents achieved is what drives successful people. Being satisfied with life by looking back to what your parents achieved is the biggest obstacle in the way of advancing in life. The past can be used as a reference point but not a determinant of your life.

The relationship was not working; in the spring of 1992, Jayke arranged to send my oldest son, Herbert, to Dallas to visit his maternal aunt. The aunt, who was visiting us in California, had a son who was about Herbert's age. The two sisters wanted the cousins to spend the summer together and get to know each other. Herbert traveled to Dallas with his aunt. At the end of summer, Jayke traveled to Dallas to bring Herbert back to California. While in Dallas, Jayke started a romantic relationship with a man in Dallas who was friends with her sister. That truly was the beginning of the end of our relationship.

# Chapter 12
## First Trip To Uganda

My older brother died, and I had to travel to Uganda to attend his funeral rites. In order to travel, I had to get travel documents from the Immigration and Naturalization Service. Once I got the documents, I put in a request at work for a month's vacation, which was also approved. Days later, I drove to the United Kingdom Embassy in Los Angeles, and I applied for a visa to travel through Britain for a connecting flight. A connecting flight through Britain was the cheapest to fly to Uganda. I also wanted to stop in Britain to visit my cousins who had immigrated to that country. I had not seen them for many years, and that was an opportunity to see them and catch up with what was happening in our lives after many years. I had the necessary travel documents, and my vacation time at work was approved, so I proceeded to buy an air ticket on British Airways.

I boarded the flight in the afternoon and flew the whole night, arriving in London early in the morning. I was leaving behind a relationship that was deep in trouble. I was deeply troubled by Jayke's actions. By that time in 1994, she had gone back to Dallas, stayed there for months, and then came back. She had admitted to me by the time to having an affair with a man she met when he went to pick up Herbert. By the time I traveled, I did not see any way the relationship could be saved. Together with her sister, she had plotted to travel to Dallas and start an affair, which was still going on at the time I left to go to Uganda.

While in the UK, I got in touch with Eva, the boyhood girlfriend I left in Uganda in 1982. It had been twelve years since we had last seen each other. There were no hard feelings between the two of us. We had both been in a relationship, and we both had children of our own. We spent time talking about the good old days when we were both teenagers and about the mutual friends we had.

Eva was single, and I was stressed by Jayke's affair with a man in Dallas. The relationship was dying, and it was a good feeling to be away talking to someone and being able to relieve some of the stress of dealing with a dying relationship. With Jayke's affair, the relationship deteriorated beyond repair.

## My Time In Uganda

I traveled to Uganda on British Airways from Heathrow Airport and arrived at Entebbe Airport in the afternoon. I had relatives waiting for me at the airport, and after we had lunch, we drove to Kampala, about thirty miles away. I spent days with my brother Joseph and his wife, Cissy. These are the people I lived with through my teenage years in Kololo while attending high school and Makerere University. We spent hours talking about all the years we had been apart and all that had happened in between.

I spent a few days in the city, after which I traveled with my brother Joseph to Masaka, where the ceremonies and the last funeral rites were to be held for my brother. It was a Friday, and the ceremonies were to be held the following day. My brother Joseph had not informed people in Masaka that I had arrived in the country. My relatives were surprised and excited to see me.

We spent the whole weekend in Masaka, returning to Kampala on a Monday evening. On returning to the city, I laid out a plan to see my old friends to catch up on old times. I met up with Fred and Mull. I learned that my other friend with whom I had spent time in college had passed on. I also visited with my other relatives in the capital and went to see some of the places that I used to patronize when I was growing up. It was a different country from the one I left behind that was war-torn. Buildings were repaired, roads were drivable, and there were no army roadblocks and checkpoints that were common before I left in 1982.

My vacation days went by fast, and soon, it was time to return to the US and leave the country that I had not seen for over twelve years. The wars had ended, and the country had turned the corner and was starting its way back to prosperity and peace. The images and thoughts I had in mind of what I was to find once I landed at Entebbe were proven wrong. It was a pleasant surprise.

## Re-Entering The US

After a couple of weeks in Uganda, I flew from Entebbe Airport and landed at London Heathrow Airport on my way back to the US. I presented my passport with a visa, and I was allowed entry into the United Kingdom. After three days, I went back to Heathrow airport, this time to board a plane back to Los Angeles.

At the check-in counter, I was questioned at length about my travel document. The parole document the US Immigration issued to me was being questioned. It allowed me to re-enter the US without a green card or US passport. The gentleman at the counter did not quite understand the validity of the document. All people boarding flights to the US were required to show an entry visa or prove that they were permitted to reside in the US. The British Airline staff took the documents from me and went to the back office. He returned after an hour and handed the documents back to me, and I continued with my check-in. No explanation was given as to why he made me wait for so long. I was relieved to get my travel papers back and did not ask questions. I checked in my luggage, and soon after, we started boarding, and the plane took off for Los Angeles.

The flight landed at LAX in the afternoon. I disembarked, got my luggage and carry-on bag, and proceeded to the immigration and customs checkpoints. During the flight, I was worried that I may not be allowed to re-enter the US with the temporary travel document. I did not know about how such documents were processed at the airport for entry or if I would be questioned again. Surprisingly, I was not asked any questions both at the immigration and the customs clearance areas. The immigration officer just glanced at the document and my passport and gestured for me to proceed to the baggage claim area. I felt relieved, for the biggest worry was that I would be denied entry.

I had decided not to tell Jayke when I was going to land at LAX. Communication between us was extremely limited by then because of the unfaithfulness that had happened. I knew all along that I had to find my transportation from the airport. I had to look for a taxicab on a sixty-five-mile drive from LAX back to Riverside. I picked up my luggage from the baggage claim and proceeded to the ground transportation area to look for a taxicab. I spoke to several taxi drivers, and I found one who was driving to Orange County and on to Riverside. The drive home took about one hour, and I arrived at my house a little after seven in the evening.

# Chapter 13
## After Jayke Left The House

Once I returned from Uganda, Jayke and I got into an argument. The following day, she left the house with all the house belongings and decided to go back to Dallas to be with her boyfriend. After she left, I slowly started rebuilding my life piece by piece, beginning with buying basic items needed for living a normal life. First, I had to find a bed, mattress, and bed sheets. Since I had a mortgage to pay and credit card debt for the items that Jayke had taken, I started off buying items from discount stores. Falling back to the lessons I learned when I first arrived in the US back in my college days, I started by looking for discounted items on sale. I bought a mattress, a bed frame, a box spring, and a microwave to begin with. For about a month, I did not have pans, pots, or utensils. Instead, I bought readymade meals from grocery stores. I did my laundry at a laundromat. After six months, I bought used appliances and connected a washer and dryer in the garage. As months went by, I bought a used dining table sofa and loveseat. Slowly, the house started looking like it was lived in.

I was content with the items I bought and had no regrets that Jayke emptied the house when she left or that I was paying the credit card bills. My focus at that time was to get back on my feet, knowing that I would rebuild my life back to normal.

I talked to the children often on the phone and we would talk about their new life in Texas and how they were doing in school. They were missing their friends they had left in California. Juliet was four years old by then and missed being with me. She had her first day going to school, catching a bus to go to school. I missed seeing her leaving on her first day of school.

When summer break came around, I arranged to have the kids come to Riverside to spend the summer break with me. I bought them tickets and had them fly unaccompanied on a JetBlue flight to Long Beach. I paid extra money to have the hostesses take care of them on the plane. When the plane landed at Long Beach airport, the hostesses handed the kids over to me. I went to the airport with a family friend whose children were friends and playmates with my children. We welcomed the kids back to California and the kids were excited to see their friends again.

Days before their arrival, I started buying more utensils, pots, and pans because I knew we were to make meals at home. Since Jayke had left the house with everything, there were no beds, mattresses, or bed coverings for the children to sleep on. I shopped for and bought mattresses, beds, covers, utensils, plates, and cups before the children arrived.

## Life As A Single Parent

I became a single dad taking care of three children, with one of them a daughter barely five years old. I learned fast to take care of young children. Apart from preparing meals and doing laundry, I had to find daycare for them. I was working five days a week and gone all day. I could not leave the children at home by themselves, especially the five-year-old daughter, who required much care. I called different daycare facilities to try to find one that was affordable. They were all out of my budget. I had a mortgage to pay, buy food for the children, pay bills, buy them clothes, and provide the children with other necessities. Their mother sent them over to California and claimed that she was unemployed, so she could not send any money. I became the only one financially responsible for the children.

One weekend, I took my car to a shop for repair, and I met a lady from Ghana who also had brought her car to the shop for service. We introduced ourselves to each other as we waited for our vehicles, and we had a brief conversation. I got to learn that she lived in Riverside and she had a young sister who had just arrived in the US. I asked if her sister could help me to babysit my children. She went home that night and talked to her sister, and she gave me a call later in the night and told me that the sister was willing to babysit. I would have to pay her on a weekly basis. We agreed on the money, and she started babysitting. She also would supervise the kids as they made their breakfast and lunch and she prepared meals for Juliet. She had no car, so I had to pick her up every morning at about 5:30 and take her back to her apartment in the evening.

I had her babysit for about a month, after which she stopped coming. She had found something else to do. I knew when I got her that she would not last long. Many people who come to the US from Africa come hungry to advance their skills and improve their earning power. That is always their top priority. I learned later that she had enrolled in Riverside Community College classes, and her schedule couldn't let her babysit.

One day in the evening, I received a call from Jayke telling me that she wanted me to keep the children in California for an extended period. She did not say why she did not want the children back in Dallas. Since she did not want the children back, I had to keep them in California, and I had to enroll them in school.

I did not have their records, such as birth certificates and immunization records, for me to enroll them. I told Jayke to mail me the records. Jayke sent them, and once I got them, I went to Ben Franklin Elementary School, and I enrolled them in classes. Juliet was old enough then, and I enrolled her in first grade. Months before, the other two children had been pulled out of the same school by their mother. The school staff enquired why, on two occasions, the children were pulled out of school and then re-enrolled months later. Without telling them my personal life I told them the children were going to be living with me.

A few days after they started classes, the school staff called me to say that Nante had fallen behind due to the classes she missed while she was being moved around different schools. The school set up a program for her to catch up and I agreed to the instruction.

The school was close to the house and within walking distance. Before I left for work every morning, I made sure they were ready for school. Juliet, the youngest, could not walk by herself; she had to walk with her older siblings. I instructed Herbert, the oldest of them, to look out for them. Nante was always protective of her little sister, even when Herbert would choose to hang out with his friends.

I had to get used to taking care of the children fast. I learned to do girls' hair, especially Juliet's hair. I had to get her ready for school every morning, making sure that her hair was nicely done. Nante had gotten good at doing her hair, and eventually, she did her younger sister's hair in the morning before school. I had to look for hair stylists when the hair needed much work that could not be done at home. Braiding the hair was the easiest way to have manageable hair because, in the morning, it would take a few minutes to get the hair to look decent for school.

Every weekend, I went with the children to the stores to shop for items that we would need for the week. The children knew what they wanted, and they would prepare a shopping list. Especially important were the items that they needed for breakfast in the morning. The mornings were always hectic, and I had to buy breakfast items that were easy to prepare so that we could leave in time for work and school.

I did all of this without financial help from their mother. As weeks went by, she finally told me why she sent the children back to California. She was pregnant and expecting a child with her boyfriend. They did not want the responsibilities of three children while they were pregnant.

I had lost a babysitter, and I had full responsibility for the children, and it was going to be for a long time. The biggest challenge was to find someone to watch them once they came home from school. I could see them off to school in the morning, but school ended at about three in the afternoon while I was still at work. They were not old enough to be by themselves at home. So, I had to take quick action to address the problem.

While attending school, the children fell sick very often. Almost every two weeks, one of them would catch a cold or a cough. I constantly gave them medications and made frequent trips to their doctor's office. Juliet, the youngest, was the most susceptible to those illnesses. I could come home and find her sneezing, coughing, or with a fever in bed sleeping. On days when she felt very sick, I would take days off work to take care of her.

I took so many days off work in a few months, and my boss called me into his office and told me to find reliable daycare. I told him I would, but I knew that was not easy to do. One morning, Juliet went to school with a cold, and I went to work. While I was at work, I got a call from the school nurse's office. The nurse said Juliet was in her office and that I had to go pick her up. She said that she needed me to go to the nurse's office when I got to the school because she wanted to talk to me.

I asked for family-sick leave at work and left at ten o'clock. When I got to the school, I found Juliet sitting in the front office. The clerk informed the school nurse and the school principal that I was at the front office. The principal came out and questioned me about the nature of parenting the kids were getting at home. She asked whether there was any other person in the house to look after the children or whether I was a single parent. She asked why Juliet was at school when she had a cold. I told her that she wasn't sick to the point where she needed to stay home. It was a common cold that children frequently got. She said that Juliet should have stayed home that day, and she threatened to call the Social Services Department. I told her that Juliet had seen a doctor the previous evening who recommended over-the-counter medication for her cold. The doctor did not feel it was a serious illness.

I felt like the principal was being sexist, for she appeared to think that because I was a male single parent, I could not take care of the children. Luckily, I never had another conversation like that with the school staff. The situation remained calm for many months, and I had been able to balance work and being a single parent taking care of the children.

Babysitting had become a serious problem that I had to address urgently, so I took a day off work to find childcare. After calling and searching different places, I found an advertisement by an employment agency in one of the local magazines. The advertisement stated that they had people looking for work as maids. I went to the agency's office to inquire about the people looking for work. In particular, I was interested in knowing if it was safe to have the person hired around children. Did the agency thoroughly screen the workers? The agency assured me that they thoroughly screened the people looking for work, including looking at their criminal background and past work history.

Several people were sitting in the office waiting to be hired. I interviewed three people the agency presented, and of the three, I hired an older woman who appeared to be in her fifties. She had previous experience taking care of little children, and I saw her fit to look after the children, especially

Juliet, who was the youngest. The maid would take care of the children from Monday to Friday and take the weekends off. She helped them with meal preparation in the morning and when they returned from school. She had to pick up Juliet on days when she could not walk back with her siblings. Herbert and Nante would walk with their friends, unlike Juliet, who still needed someone to pick her up. On days when the children walked back home by themselves, the maid was home to receive them.

Weeks went by, and the maid quit the job, and I had no babysitter, so, again, I started looking for maids. I called the employment agency to get another maid, and the agency did not have anyone available to start work immediately. On our street, there was a single parent who tragically had lost her husband in an accident. Every morning, I saw her walk her two little girls to the same school my children attended. I had talked to her once, but she mostly kept to herself. That evening, I went and knocked on her door, and I introduced myself as the neighbor living a few houses across the street. I told her that I had three kids at the house and that I go to work every morning. I asked her if she could look after my children when they came home from school to see that nothing wrong was happening at the house. She agreed to my request. I told the children that if they needed anything or if anything happened while I was not home, they could go to her house. For all the time she accepted that responsibility, there were no incidents that happened. The kids were well-behaved, and the lady never had to deal with any issues. The arrangement I had with the neighbor was acceptable for children who were as old as mine.

The children adjusted well to the arrangement, and they were always home by themselves for a few hours after school before I got home. They would do their homework and once I returned, I would check their homework and answer any questions or help them with the hard problems. Juliet was too young to do homework by herself, so in the evening, I would help with it. Looking back at how the neighbor helped, I now see how relevant the saying "It takes a village to raise a child" is true.

Summer of 1995 came, and I still had the children in Riverside, waiting for Jayke to accept them back in Dallas. By then, we had settled into a family routine, all of us knowing how to deal with the life we had. That summer, Eva arranged to take a vacation from her job in the UK to travel to the United States. She told me she would be traveling to the US and spend three weeks, and she wanted to come by and visit me while she was in the US. I let her proceed with her arrangements. She spent time at the house, and she got to meet the children.

The children were well-established in school and had reconnected with their friends. However, I didn't have legal authority to keep them in California, and I knew well that, at any time, Jayke could drive back to California, pull them out of school, and take them back to Texas. She had pulled them out of school two times before, so it was likely that she could do it the third time. Her previous actions had caused them to miss school and fall behind other students of their age. She believed that the children belonged to her and that only she was the one to make important decisions that affected their lives. To her, I had no right to decide on what they should do or what school to attend. In her mind, she alone had all the right to make those decisions.

I didn't share her beliefs, and I considered children's education to be more important than anything else. I therefore consulted with an attorney to inquire about my rights as a parent. I was particularly interested in knowing how to stop Jayke from pulling the children out of school in the middle of the school year. She was starting to make it a habit with no regard for the children's future and education.

The attorney advised that, legally, nothing would stop Jayke from pulling the children out of school. The only way to stop her from taking the children from state to state, from one school to another, was to get a court order specifying where the children should reside and attend school.

As the parent concerned about the children's future, I had to act to ensure that they got an education. Whatever misunderstandings we had between us as parents, they were not to ruin the children's future. Their education was of paramount importance. The attorney advised me to go to family court and get an order spelling out where the children would reside and attend school and each parent's responsibilities and rights. He pointed out the courts tend to favor mothers in custody cases but because of Jayke's previous actions, I had a good chance the court would rule in my favor.

I instructed the attorney to file a custody case in Riverside Family Court and have Jayke served with papers in Texas. I was advised not to alert her before she was served with the summons. If she had become aware before being served, she could have taken the children out of California before the trial.

The attorney arranged for the summons papers to be sent to Dallas, and Jayke was served. When that day for the court appearance came, we both showed up at the courthouse. My attorney represented me, and he explained the reasons why I asked for custody. He told the court how the children had missed many days of school and how they were moved from one school to another in the middle of the school year. Jayke argued that she had legal custody rights and that the children were only visiting me in California. She was reminded that there was no court order giving her custody of the children.

We were each asked to explain our living arrangements for the children. I had a four-bedroom house, and each child could have a bedroom. Jayke, on the other hand, was in a two-bedroom apartment she shared with her boyfriend and their newborn. The judge was not convinced that Jayke had sufficient housing for the additional three children.

While addressing the judge, Jayke spent much of her time telling the court the reasons why she wanted to take the children back to Texas. She made all sorts of false accusations about me, telling the judge how I was not a good parent and that I had mistreated the children. She accused Eva of abusing the children even though Eva had not spent much time with the children. The court found no merit in her arguments that I was not fit to be a parent. The children were living with me, and I had taken care of them without her help whatsoever for over a year. I paid for all their school expenses and provided them with a decent house to live in. I had done all that without any child support money coming from Jayke. She was a deadbeat parent.

After Jayke made outrageous accusations of how I was mistreating the children, the judge ordered that we show up the following morning in a Temecula courtroom. The judge ordered me to bring the children with me. At the time, Jayke had an infant, and she showed up at the courthouse with her boyfriend and the newborn at the hearing.

At the courthouse, the children were separated from us by the court staff. I proceeded to the courtroom, and when my case came up, the judge said she had ordered the court mediator to interview the children and present the court with a report of findings. She was to investigate the accusations Jayke made in court the day before. The court mediator also talked to me and Jayke and interviewed us to tell our side of the story.

After a lunch break, we went back into the courtroom and our case was called by the judge. The court mediator had already presented her report of findings to the court. The judge started by commending me for taking good care of the children for the previous twelve months. She talked about the findings of the court mediator. She stated how the children had been interviewed separately and how no negative findings were included in the report. All of Jayke's accusations were not corroborated in the children's interviews. The children had also been asked about their preference of where they wanted to reside.

The judge gave me primary physical custody and ordered that they attend school in California. Legal custody was to be shared, and children were not to be transferred from one state to another without both of us agreeing. They could spend school breaks with their mother if she bought air tickets for them to travel to and from Dallas. Jayke was ordered to pay child support. She ignored the child support order, and within three months, she was a deadbeat parent. I raised the three children on my income without her help. To date, she still owes the child support money that the court ordered.

The court also ordered that we not engage in spreading malicious rumors about each other and not to say negative things about each other in the presence of the children. Again, Jayke ignored the judge's order and continued spreading malicious lies about me. She engaged in a campaign to poison the children's mindsets by depicting me as a terrible person.

As a family, we were ordered to attend counseling sessions with a marriage, family, and child counselor to address issues of joint parenting. I paid for all the sessions, and I took all the children to the sessions which were held in Riverside. Jayke did not come to the counseling sessions. The counselor concluded that the children were being well cared for, and she gave us advice on how to deal with each other regarding parenting issues.

The court proceedings were stressful for everyone, and I could see from the children's faces. I intended to ensure that the kids had a decent education and a stable home. I had no problem sending them to visit her in Dallas since now I had the law behind me, had Jayke decided to keep them in Texas. She came to court claiming how she cared so much about the children; however, only once over the many years did she send air tickets for them to go and spend school breaks or holidays with her.

Like the comments made by the judge, the family counselor emphasized to us as parents to refrain from attacking each other with negative statements. Such attacks would have negative effects on the children. Their mother never followed that advice as she continued to attack me with all sorts of lies and negative information. She made untrue statements to the children and other people she talked to. I took the high road and chose to follow the judge's and counselor's advice for the good of the children. I did not engage in vengeful attacks against her, for I knew it would be the children who would end up being negatively affected.

What followed the court hearing was a feeling of calm because everyone knew exactly what to expect. The children knew where they were supposed to go to school and when they could go for visits. I continued to take care of them and continued to pay for all of their expenses and their everyday needs. I find it surprising that now that they are adults and have jobs and careers, she wants to be so much in their lives. She continues to fabricate stories and distort facts to make her look like she is a caring parent, ignoring the fact that she never gave the children any financial support.

# Chapter 14

## My Start In Real Estate

On my flight to the US in 1982, I had thoughts running through my mind of what I could do to reach millionaire status and how I could help my family members have a better life. Those ideas never faded even as I went through college and started working. Raising a family, holding down a job, and being the sole earner for the family made my goals seem unattainable. I was determined to achieve my dreams, and my determination became even stronger after I went through difficult experiences in my personal life and in the workplace.

To this effect, I tried out many things that I thought would make me earn extra money on the side as I worked my regular job to support my family. There used to be infomercials on late-night television looking for people who wanted to earn money by assembling items. The infomercials had telephone numbers to call to get started. I ordered kits with parts to assemble and send back for merchants to sell. At night after work and after I had helped the children with their homework, and on weekends, I assembled pieces of jewelry and crafts. The kits came with assembly instructions, and after I assembled them, I sent them back to the merchants. The companies set standards that I had to meet to have the assembled items accepted. The company accepted some of them and rejected others that were sent back to me with comments on how to improve the assembly. As I assembled more items, I got at it and started getting paid for my work.

To earn a substantial amount of money required assembling many pieces that had to be accepted. I was doing the work on weekends and at night after my regular day job, and I realized that since I was not assembling items full-time, earning large amounts of money was not going to be possible. So, I continued to search for other ways to bring in money to supplement my city job income to support the family. I formed a company to do planning and design work. I was aware of the strict regulations restricting government employees from engaging in private work. The regulations require filing a conflict-of-interest disclosure form listing businesses and financial interests located within the City of Riverside. Every year, I filed a State of California Conflict of Interest form, disclosing that I was not working on projects within the City of Riverside boundaries. My strategy was to look for individuals who needed planning or design services located outside of the city. That way, I would eliminate the appearance of a conflict of interest. I focused on work that I could do in my free time and did not require visiting offices during the week. I called my newly formed company, HKM Associates.

When I went to conferences and business gatherings, I handed out business cards for my company to attract clients. I was competing with companies and individuals who were working full-time on planning and design projects. They had more time dedicated to their clients' work as well as I worked part-time. I drew interest from several individuals who wanted entitlements to add to their residences and needed their building plans approved by cities and the county. Soon, I realized that if I didn't devote all my time to working for HKM Associates, I would not be able to attract enough clients to generate money to live on. That required complete dedication to the business.

For years, I had seen television commercials, such as the Carlton Sheets, which explained how one could build wealth by investing in real estate. I was intrigued by what they were advocating, so I decided to explore more about how those real estate programs worked. They sounded like the programs fit my situation and would help me reach my goals. I also knew that there were many complaints about how companies advertising wealth creation defrauded people. I decided to try out those companies myself while taking a lot of precautions at the same time. Without spending money, I ordered printed materials from Carlton Sheets. The printed material talked about building wealth in real estate with no money down.

Some of the schemes Carlton Sheets explained appeared to make sense, while others seemed very suspect. To use the schemes described in the printed material, one had to buy additional material and attend training courses. I decided not to buy the material. The free introductory material, however, gave me additional motivation, and I continued looking for other ways to make money in real estate but with less risk.

It was 1997, and I had welcomed a son with Eva, who had emigrated to America, and the family size had grown. She had a pre-teen daughter from a previous relationship when we got married, so there were five children in the house. We were living in a four-bedroom, three-bathroom house and as the children grew older, the house became small for the family.

They were constantly arguing about who was to use the shower first and who got to make breakfast ahead of who. They were quickly approaching college age, and I was about to start paying their college expenses. I had to come up with solutions to what was starting to appear like a mountain of problems ahead.

I searched college catalogs published quarterly by Southern California schools for real estate courses. The University of California in Riverside (UCR) and Riverside Community College (RCC) published catalogs outlining classes in many fields, including real estate. They were mostly offered in the evenings and weekends and were open to anyone. Those classes were to be my avenue into real estate investing. I had found my calling.

I started investing in real estate to build wealth, to be able to send my children to college, and to take my mind off the frustrations at my job. I had worked for the city and had been passed over for promotions to top positions even when I trained people who were promoted, and those people were made my boss. I wrote reports, and before they were published, someone else would remove my name and claim to be the author even though all they did was review the report.

Real estate was a great way to invest since I could juggle training classes, seminars, and city work. It is often referred to as "armchair investing" because you can do it sitting in your living room. I could look for investments, conduct due diligence, and communicate with brokers and property managers on the Internet without traveling to far places.

I looked for properties to buy and researched various aspects of the property online. I could view the property's interior and exterior, do a street view of the neighborhood, research schools, check crime statistics, and see what stores were in the area. The information contained in the census data provides details on any given area or neighborhood. The website provided me with neighborhood information on things like income levels, the age of the population, levels of education, and the cost of housing. I could also get information on the real estate sales, including the number of homes sold and how much they sold for. The information made it easy for me to compare properties to buy. It fitted the name given to it, "Armchair Investing."

I took a college class in real estate finance and development during my college years. However, I needed to know what was happening in the real investing world. Thus, I needed further training by attending weekend and evening classes and seminars. I had bought a house and gone through the buying process, but I had to build up my knowledge and confidence further. I was to sign documents and commit to holding properties that were to tie me down financially for a long time. The knowledge I had accumulated attending the training helped me to make the decision to keep the first home I bought in 1992, which turned into a rental house after I bought a bigger house in 2003.

By 2000, my focus on further climbing the career ladder at the City of Riverside had mostly disappeared, and I had rearranged my priorities. I had been denied career advancements, and instead, those opportunities went to young, more recent graduates whom I coached to do the job. Additionally, I was paired with other top management staff, with whom I educated on how the department and city functioned. I had complained about discrimination, and I had concluded that laws on the books didn't do much to stop social injustice. It was clear to me that the job was not going to be the avenue to take to achieve what I believed to be my personal accomplishments. It was time to refocus entirely and come up with ideas that I could implement to reach my goals and be able to educate my children. My education, job knowledge, and other professional qualifications did not matter when it came to promotions. I had to keep working, and I held on to the job at least up to the time non-job-related income could be enough to cover my expenses.

Real estate provided the perfect avenue to achieve my goals since there were many ways I could earn money without spending much time being actively involved. I could divide my time between the job and investing. I spent my free time looking for real estate investing opportunities while I worked at my regular job.

## Riverside Community College Classes

The initial classes I took were at UCR and were offered on Saturday mornings. I then discovered classes offered at RCC taught on the weekends. Some of the classes lasted the whole day, while others were only in the morning. I found classes taught by Marshall Reddick to be informative, and they covered many areas of real estate investing in detail. Marshall's weekend classes cost less than $100, and they were held on several community college campuses throughout Southern California. They were perfect for my job schedule and left time for me to spend time with the children.

The first two sessions I attended were taught by Marshall Reddick himself, who founded the Marshall Reddick Real Estate Network. He introduced himself as a retired economics professor at California State University Los Angeles. He had published several books and pamphlets that had information on many aspects of real estate investing. The information included demographics, historical trends in real estate, and economies of different areas of the country. There was also information about realtors, property managers, and lenders in different parts of the country.

The courses covered different real estate investment strategies, including how to buy a first investment property, how to build a team, how to buy out-of-state properties, how to rehabilitate properties, how to buy foreclosures, where and how to find them, and tax laws as they related to real estate investment. He described his journey to becoming a successful real estate investor. He explained how he held a W-2 job and decided to use real estate to achieve financial success.

His story made an impression on me, and I saw myself in his place. I pictured myself following his path from being a regular nine-to-five employee to owning several properties that generated enough income for me and my family. The instructors recommended that at the beginning, it was important to have a mentor for guidance until one developed the skills to invest.

One afternoon, after the class, we went on a tour of bank-owned properties for sale. We walked through those properties and discussed the opportunities each house possessed and how to submit offers to the banks. We were also advised on how to rehabilitate the home after the purchase, focusing on the after-repair values as the key to making a decision. On the following weekends, I attended more seminars dealing with different aspects of real estate.

Real estate investing is one of the fields where minority groups are underrepresented. In the classes, I used to be the only black person, and I had to get used to people staring at me with looks that appeared to wonder what I was doing in such a class. There was a belief that real estate investing was not something that black people do.

Twenty years later, I now see black people in the real estate seminars and conferences that I attend. I was a black person who immigrated to the US and the expectations of being a real estate investor were low. Some Ugandan acquaintances were equally suspicious and did not believe that I could invest in real estate. I told one Ugandan that I was focused on investing in real estate in different states. He did not believe that I could accomplish such a task. He believed that real estate investing was for white people, who he assumed had the money. As immigrants of color, we need to believe in ourselves and start investing in real estate. If we believe that we can invest in real estate and be successful, we can harvest the fruits that real estate investing brings.

In the classes, Marshall mentioned that he had formed real estate investment clubs that met in different cities throughout

California. After attending his classes at Riverside Community College (RCC), I went to a club meeting in Riverside on a Thursday evening. The club did not require money to join or start investing, unlike many other clubs which required payment of high fees, sometimes in thousands of dollars to join. The club meetings offered investment opportunities and a chance to implement investment strategies that were taught in the classes. Real estate brokers and loan officers made presentations to attendees, trying to sell them homes and loans.

## Local Club Meetings

Still with apprehension, I continued to attend local club meetings in Riverside and neighboring cities like Corona and Rancho Cucamonga in the evenings. I recall entering a room full of people and different speakers walking up the podium to talk about homes they had for sale. Their presentations were impressive, with photographs, economic data about the areas, schools, and other demographic information. I got a deeper insight into what real estate investing was all about. Several speakers talked about how they started in real estate investing and their experiences, mistakes, and achievements. I came to realize that many people were like me. They started with little or no experience in real estate investing, and they had regular W-2 jobs. Seeing such people I could relate to made me more confident to pursue real estate investing. The club meetings provided plenty of information on investing strategies, how to start, what pitfalls to avoid, and areas of the country most likely to have high appreciation rates and which ones were landlord friendly.

## Choosing An Investment Strategy

I had gained enough knowledge to start actively investing. From the classes and seminars, I learned of strategies to invest in single-family residences, duplexes, fourplexes, and multi-family residences. Of the many strategies taught in the classes, I chose to start with the buy-and-hold. I put my efforts into finding and buying a new house to live in but keep my four-bedroom, three-bath home I bought in 1992. From the classes, I learned that the four-bedroom, three-bathroom homes were the ones that were most in demand by renters. Many young families with young school-going children preferred to rent such homes over homes with fewer bedrooms and bathrooms.

I focused on looking for properties in the area close to home in Riverside, California. One of the things I learned from the classes was to decide whether to buy properties to hold for appreciation or to generate positive cash flow every month. A cash flow strategy would not work in California, where homes are expensive. So, choosing to invest in California would not be going for cash flow. Investing for cash flow meant looking in cheaper states with cheaper homes but high rents, such as Texas and Florida. Texas had cheap properties and at the same time, the rents from those homes were quite high. That allowed for positive cash flow every month after paying the mortgage and miscellaneous expenses.

## Foreclosed Homes Strategy

As I searched for the appropriate strategy, I evaluated investing in foreclosed properties. I knew that those properties were, in many cases, sold at a discount compared to others not in distress. I put my name on a list to get a list of foreclosed properties from real estate brokers in neighboring cities. Every couple of weeks I would get a list of bank-repossessed homes mailed to me that were up for sale. I would visit the properties to see the condition they were in from the exterior.

On some occasions, the brokers would let me see the inside of the house. Many of the homes I toured required extensive repairs, and at that time, I did not have the money to rehabilitate them and put them back on the market for sale. The strategy required much cash available to fund the repairs. I also did not find anyone who convinced me that they were very knowledgeable in investing in repossessed homes to mentor me and show me the ropes on how it is done. Without anyone to counsel me, all I saw were these huge problems with each of the properties that I visited.

Looking back now, I see how I missed out on some of the opportunities that would have been profitable. In the field of real estate, finding a mentor does not come easy, especially for minorities, let alone someone who immigrated to this country. The perceptions society has about people who look like me were hard to overcome. A good mentor has to have trust in you and be willing to spend time with the mentee, showing them how to get started investing and holding them by the hand for the initial years. The general perception was immigrants from Africa could not possibly invest in real estate. Having money is not associated with people of African origin. Such stereotypical perceptions still exist and do affect many immigrants. That did not deter me from pursuing my dreams.

I continued looking around for ways to educate myself further and searching for properties to buy.

## Finding A Bigger Family Home

I had firmly decided that real estate investing was the way to gain financial independence. It would also give me a sense of satisfaction that I was using my free time away from work fruitfully. By 2000, the children were growing, and their needs were changing. I started thinking of finding a bigger home that had more bedrooms than the four-bedroom house that we were living in. I knew that if I had bought a rental property first, it would have been difficult to buy a new primary home with more rooms. The strategy, therefore, was to look and buy a bigger primary home first and figure out how to turn the four-bedroom house we lived in into a rental house.

Looking for a new home was a family affair; I involved the children throughout the search. We found a house close to where we lived. It was in a nice, gated community that was under construction. I visited the sales office and filled out an application to be pre-qualified. At the time, homes were selling very fast. Before my application was processed for qualification, all the homes in the subdivision were sold.

Because I was working in the Planning Department, I knew that there was a subdivision nearby that was being processed through city approvals. The subdivision was next to the gated community where I had missed out on the houses. After a few months, the developer was approved to start construction work on the subdivision. It was a perfect location for it was next to the gated community and close to the home I was living in. It was being developed by the same company that built homes in the gated community. The builder specialized in building luxury, semi-custom homes.

Soon after securing the permits, the developer started advertising the future homes by putting out "Coming Soon" advertisements. When I missed out on buying into the gated community, I signed up to be notified when the list of prospective buyers started forming. At that time, the site was a vacant piece of land with rock outcroppings, but I knew that it would eventually be developed with homes. The subdivision map had been approved by the city but had not yet been recorded with the County Recorder. The owner had to first satisfy certain conditions of approval. So, there was some risk that the lot I wanted to buy could not end up the way it appeared on the tentative map that had been approved.

I received a call from the developer that the lots in the subdivision were up for sale and that they were taking deposits from prospective buyers. The subdivision had only 29 lots so I knew they would be sold out very quickly. I went into the sales office and picked a lot to buy; by that time, almost 13 lots had been bought. The subdivision was in the same school district as the residence we lived in; thus, the children would not change schools. There would not be any interruption in their education.

At that time, my primary objective as far as children's education was concerned was to have them in the same schools until they went on to the next level of education. One of the daughters was in middle school and the following year would be in high school. The youngest son was in preschool and would attend a school close to the house. They had been through enough school changes in their earlier years, and I had realized how switching schools had affected them negatively. They could have fallen behind in their studies and would have struggled to catch up.

By the time I put down a deposit for the lot, the area of the future homes was vacant, and there were no model homes to visit. The developer had built homes that had a similar floor plan about ten miles away. The salesperson advised me that if I wanted to see models, I would have to go to that development. I drove the ten miles with the kids in tow to see what our future house would look like. The children were excited to see the home. They started assigning themselves rooms even before the construction of our home had begun. The homes were semi-custom, and as a buyer, I had the option of changing the floor plan to suit the family's living needs. On the exterior, I made no major changes, but inside, I rearranged the floor plan by moving the walls around and came up with a different floor plan configuration. I increased the number of bedrooms and added bathrooms for each of the bedrooms. It cost more money for the alterations and add-ons, but that is what the family needed.

The model home I toured with the children was a 4-bedroom house with a large bar, entertainment room with a giant piano area, and space for band instruments. It was designed to hold live band music if the owner wanted to do so. We, as a family, did not need a bar or a concert room. We instead needed more bedrooms and bathrooms where each of the children would have their self-contained rooms. I spent time with the developer and reworked the floor plan to come up with a dream house. I ended up having six-bedroom rooms with five and a half bathrooms. With each of the bedrooms having its own bathroom, the children would not fight to use the bathrooms in the morning as they prepared to go to school. Arguing about who would go first was a constant problem in the four-bedroom that we occupied.

Construction on the site began three months after I put down a deposit to buy the lot. I drove by the site daily in the morning to work after I dropped off the children at school. I could see the construction in progress. First, it was the giant earthmovers being brought and parked on the vacant rocky site. My heart was filled with excitement, for I was starting to see signs that my dream was about to happen. Within weeks the brushes and sparse citrus trees that dotted the land were removed by the giant graders. That was followed soon after by the grading trucks moving dirt.

Soon I started seeing roads being curved out of the vacant site. At first, they looked like just driving trails used by the graders to move the dirt around. But eventually, they started to look like real roads for I could see future streets curve and turns and cul-de-sacs being rounded off. Then, demarcations of the lots themselves started to appear, with stakes being placed along the streets under construction. The lot I picked was further away from the existing paved street. But I had a good idea of where the lot was located and where my house would be built.

## Raising Money For A Down Payment And Closing Costs

As the months went by and the construction progressed, I could see the concrete slabs that formed the house floors then I started seeing the wood frames go up. It was time to focus on the money that I would need to buy the house. How was I going to come up with the money for the down payment and closing costs? In the training classes and seminars, there was a discussion of how to become a real estate investor, and one of the ways was to convert a primary house into a rental house to generate rental income. My first home had appreciated in value with a lot of equity built up.

I refinanced the loan on the house and took out money to start my journey as a real estate investor. I got enough money to use as a down payment and pay the closing costs on the new house. In the middle of March 2004, I was invited to walk through the house to see the progress. By then, the house needed a few items to be installed, but the major systems and appliances were all already installed. The flooring had not yet been finished, and the walls were not yet painted.

As the closing of escrow approached, the escrow company asked me to set up a day and time when I could sign the closing papers. At the end of March 2004, I walked into the escrow company office in Ontario, California, signed the escrow papers, and became the owner of two homes.

My loan application made it clear that I intended to keep the primary home I had as a rental house. To close on the new house, I had to prove that the rental income I was going to collect would be sufficient to cover the mortgage of the converted rental home with money left over for expenses and reserves. I got comparable rental values in the area, which the lender had asked to see as proof that the rent collected was enough. The loan papers were signed on the new home, and I became a real estate investor.

## Sweat Equity/Landscaping The Yards

After I moved into my new primary residence, I continued educating myself in more complex ways of investing. The one thing I decided to do was to save money so I could acquire more houses. Saving on expenses stood out as the avenue available immediately through which I could save. There were many tasks that I knew how to do and where I could start saving by utilizing the concept of sweat equity. The home I had just bought was without landscaping. I knew how to design an irrigation system and how to install it. I did the work myself and that saved me thousands of dollars. I took vacation days to work on the improvements, completing the work in two months.

## Renovating Silvercrest

I was aware that I would have to spend money to fix up the home and convert it into a rental to get it ready for tenants. The classes I attended taught me how to renovate homes, so I knew how to look for, screen, and hire contractors. I also knew how to estimate renovation costs. Soon after I closed on the new house, I started looking for contractors to do the repairs. The interior was upgraded to make the house competitive in the rental market. A new carpet was installed, as well as a new floor tile, new window blinds, new countertops, new paint, and new light fixtures. The landscaping was refurbished by putting in new sod and repairing the sprinklers. The trees were trimmed, and new shrubs were planted. The appliances were replaced with new ones and the house looked like new.

## Finding a Property Manager

I decided against being actively involved in the day-to-day activities of the rental, so I looked for a property manager. The manager would screen tenants, collect rent, and deal with tenant calls for needed repairs. I wanted to use my time to engage in other more productive activities, like educating myself further by attending real estate classes. I still had a job I had to go to every morning and where I spent a whole day until evening. On top of that, I had to continue being a parent. My time was better used by paying a property manager. Having a property manager comes with the advantage that they are professionals, and that is what they do for a living. They are knowledgeable of the laws and rules governing landlord/tenant relationships.

I chose a local company that specializes in managing single-family residential properties. After I negotiated and signed a management agreement, the home was advertised, and within a few days, it was rented. I became a landlord for the first time. It was a new endeavor in which I had no prior hands-on experience except for what I had learned in the classes. The rent was high enough to pay the mortgage, and there was money left over for incidental repairs and building a reserve fund. I did not have to add money I earned from my work paycheck to operate the rental property. I learned from my real estate classes how to calculate the costs of holding a rental house, and I knew how to structure my finances.

The tenant was moving from Los Angeles and wanted a bigger house to share with her teenage boy. Everything worked out well because even before I paid my first mortgage on the new house, I had a tenant paying me rent. The money I had set aside to cover the vacancy went toward shoring up the reserve fund. To be a successful landlord, one must have sufficient reserves to cover the vacancies and unexpected repair costs. Knowing that I resisted the urge to use the money to buy furniture for the new house.

Turning my house into a rental was a good way to transition into being a landlord. I learned how to deal with tenants and how to manage property managers, a skill that later was useful. The house was close to my new home, and I could drive by to see how the tenants were maintaining the property. I was concerned about how the house would be cared for by the tenants. That was a property in which a lot of money was tied, and I still had a strong emotional attachment. Eventually, I learned to be comfortable with the fact that I could have tenants in the house without ending up with a totally damaged house.

California laws do not allow a landlord to show up at the rented house unannounced to see how the rental is being cared for. A twenty-four-hour notice to the tenants is required. The property manager inspected the house every so often to assess how the tenant was taking care of it. Every six months I would get an updated inspection report showing the condition of the house and pointing out anything that he thought was broken and needed repair. Frequent inspections enabled me to avoid having a small repair job growing into a future big problem.

## Becoming A Landlord And Fulfilling My Dreams

Owning a new home and a rental property relieved some of the frustration I had from not getting the promotion I wanted at work. The sacrifice I made to use my free time to attend real estate seminars and classes was finally paying off. I started feeling a sense of accomplishment; I finally had an investment property. I had achieved something I had wanted for many years, dating back to the days when I was a student.

When I took a class in graduate school on real estate finance and development, I had little knowledge of US real estate, and that class introduced me to real estate terms and practices. The class covered the different government agencies involved in real estate lending, like the Federal National Mortgage Association (FANNIE MAE), the Federal Home Loan Mortgage Corporation (FREDDIE MAC), the Department of Housing and Urban Development (HUD), the Department of Veterans Affairs (VA), etc., and the role they played in the real estate market. The real estate terminology was all new to me, just like the methods used to finance properties. Also, I was introduced to different methods to perform financial analysis of investment properties.

It met twice a week and started at six-thirty in the morning. That was a difficult time of the day to sit in class. I used to stay up late in the night studying, and I would struggle to keep my attention in class. The class instruction involved performing financial calculations relating to the rate of return on investment, capitalization rates, cash-on-cash return, internal rate of return, and so on. The class reinforced what my parents used to say when I was young: that real estate was a good investment and a sure way to build wealth. In 2004, when I became a real estate investor with a rental house, I was, in effect, implementing some of the investing principles I learned in that morning class. I started using the tax breaks that the tax code affords real estate investors.

## Co-Workers' Reaction

My co-workers soon learned of my decision to become a real estate investor. I heard many opinions and plenty of unsolicited advice. People's opinions were varied, many of them negative. There were people who tried to convince me that investing in rental homes was not a good idea. They pointed out the difficulties in making money in real estate and that they believed that real estate investments were scams.

There were those whose comments implied that foreign-born people were easy victims of such schemes. They tried hard to dissuade me from investing in real estate. However, my mind was not changed. I believed in myself, knowing that I had acquired enough knowledge not to be scammed. I did not pay much attention to their opinions. Instead, I continued educating myself by going to weekend and evening classes and club meetings. It is always important to stick to your investment plan and avoid advice from people who barely have knowledge of what you are trying to accomplish. After all, you spend a lot of time researching and educating yourself before you put your investment plan into place.

I credit the education I got for helping me stick to my decision because I had more knowledge of real estate than my co-workers. From club meetings, I gathered real estate-related information on different parts of the country. I was aware that real estate investing has pitfalls, but then what other investment strategy can you engage in that is risk-free? Uninvested money doesn't grow, and with inflation constantly present, that money loses value, and over time, it becomes less than what it was prior.

Investing has a risk/reward curve, and the steeper the curve, the greater the rewards. In my mind, investing in real estate was a lesser risk than putting money in individual stocks. I considered the risk curve to be less steep than that of stock investing. I also found much more satisfaction and peace of mind in investing in real estate. I always had a good feeling when every so often I drove by the properties I owned. As a counterargument to my co-workers who urged me not to invest in real estate, I pointed out to them that I could drive through the city and point to investments I owned. On the other hand, they drove around the city and could only point to projects whose plans they had processed through city reviews. They had no ownership of those properties.

Ironically, after years of owning my rental homes and after the investments appeared to be profitable, those same coworkers who tried to talk me out of buying investment properties were the same people who could not give me any credit for what I had achieved. They instead argued that someone else was responsible for buying those properties. They could not admit that they were wrong in their preconceived assumptions.

It was difficult for them to envision that I found nice properties in nice neighborhoods, arranged for their financing, and ended up owning the homes. In fact, out of jealousy, some even began to suggest that I may have used corrupt ways to buy the homes, especially those homes that were located within the City of Riverside.

Their beliefs couldn't have been any further from the truth. In California, real estate transactions are public records. There was no way that I could have been able to take bribes at work to buy those homes. If there was any corruption, it could have been easily found.

Apart from being easy to trace the sources of money involved in real estate transactions, as a city employee, the projects I worked on had to go through public reviews before they were approved. All information related to those projects was in the public domain. With all the information being public and development projects having to go through levels of reviews in different city departments, it was not possible to take any bribes. Final decisions on the project approvals were made by more than one individual and often at the highest level in the city. I took the negative comments that I heard to be sour grapes; these were people that I was now beating by miles when it came to owning investment properties. Their dire predictions that I would fail were proven wrong.

They came to realize that my weekend and evening hours were well spent educating myself on how to invest. In addition, I took an interest in knowing how real estate developers run their businesses. I talked to people who came to the city to get their projects approved, some of whom were real estate developers and investors. The difference between me and my coworkers was that I took the initiative to learn new things from those investors and developers. Some of what I learned from those investors and developers is what I used to build my real estate investment portfolio. Seeing what those investors did and the pride they showed discussing their real estate investments gave me additional inspiration to focus on real estate.

When I started investing, my primary goal was to build wealth. My secondary goal was to be able to generate enough income from real estate so that I could quit my job. I was focusing on generating enough income to replace income from the city job, income that would suffice to pay for all my living expenses and college expenses for my children. On October 9, 2014, I retired from the city job and started spending more time on my investments. I had regained my independence and was in control of how I used my time.

# Chapter 15

## Buying More Rental Homes

After living in the new house for one year, and after saving enough money and attending many more seminars, classes, and club meetings, I decided to start looking for more rental properties to buy. In the seminars and classes, there was always an emphasis on carefully choosing the areas to invest in. I learned how to analyze data to compare area economic indicators, rents, school performance, and employment growth. I used that knowledge to scrutinize the economic data, demographics, schools, and crime rates from different states in search of a suitable area to invest in. I paid much attention to what the data showed as to what might happen to an area in the coming decade. Predictions were made by looking at the demographic trends regarding income growth, income levels, economic activity, and levels of education. I narrowed my analysis to areas where the data showed growing trends in population, jobs, and incomes.

I also considered areas where I could see myself retiring or areas where I had relatives. I had screened areas in Oregon along the Pacific Ocean, a place that was a favorite for Californians who were looking for coastal living but with a relatively low cost of living. There were properties that were right along the ocean that I looked at, but I chose not to buy them because the rental market was not strong. The area appeared to be a good location to own a second home where I could go and spend a summer vacation. To an investor like me who was starting out, that luxury was not possible. I was looking for properties that would generate income and where I could use that same income to pay the mortgage on the property.

I switched my search to the State of Florida, which I knew attracted many California retirees and was landlord-friendly. Several real estate brokers had made presentations at club meetings of homes in residential subdivisions that were on sale. The homes were new, with a minimum of three bedrooms and two bathrooms, and they fit the criteria I followed to choose investment properties.

## Choosing Riverside Vs Other States

After all consideration, I chose to buy my next rental investment in Riverside. I stayed close to home while further building confidence in investing in rental properties. I also knew from working at city hall that there were subdivisions in the same neighborhood that were under construction and had some good, decent homes. That was public information available to everyone.

I decided to buy in a housing tract that was located two and a half miles from my home. In addition to single-family homes, there were areas set aside for new schools, shopping centers, and public parks. I knew the area quite well since I had worked on development projects in the neighborhood for many years. I had seen the area transform from citrus groves to a sea of red tile roofs covering single-family residences and shopping centers, office buildings, schools, and associated parking lots.

The advantages of buying and holding on to rental properties by that time were starting to be evident. It was only two years prior when I had gotten money out of the home I bought as my first home. I had used money from that house to buy a new primary residence, and there was money left over for a downpayment on a second rental home. In addition, the first rental had positive cash flow, which I was saving. I used the leftover money I had taken out at refinance and the savings to buy the second rental house. By that time, my strategy was quite simple:

- Focus On Buying Single-Family Residences With At Least Three Bedrooms And Two Bathrooms,
- Look To Buy In New Subdivision Housing Tracts,
- If Possible, Buy In The First Phase Of The Subdivision,
- Buy In Areas With Strong Economic Data, Such As High Employment Rates And Growth,
- Buy In Medium-High To High-Income Areas,
- Look For Areas With Rising Rents,
- Buy In Areas With Good Performing Schools, In Areas With A Growing Population, And Especially With Young School-Going Children,
- And Look For Areas With A Low Crime Rate.

The house I chose to buy was still under construction and would not be completed until after six months. I applied for loans from a couple of lenders to compare loan conditions. In the end, I went with the builder's preferred lender after negotiating and winning discounts and upgrades that were not offered by the other lender.

## Buying Out-Of-State Properties

By the end of 2005, I owned two rental houses with three years of experience being a landlord, and I was looking to invest more money in real estate. Both rental homes were in Riverside, close to my residence. I had focused on the area near me because of the attractive housing environment that existed. The area was growing fast, attracting high-income households whose earnings were above the state median incomes. Many of the people moving into the neighborhood were relocating from Los Angeles and Orange counties, where they held good-paying jobs. The schools were ranking high on state tests, and they were newly built with excellent teaching facilities. Commercial, office, and apartment buildings were springing up in the neighboring Mission Grove neighborhood. The former March Airforce Base was targeted for redevelopment with industrial and commercial buildings. The economic indicators showed that the redevelopment of the former Air Force base would bring in hundreds of thousands of jobs. All indications were that the area was destined for super-high growth.

Equipped with the knowledge I acquired from the real estate classes, I embarked on diversifying my investments by looking for properties in other areas away from Riverside and out of California. I considered having rental properties in different areas to be an insurance policy against economic downturns that could have occurred in Riverside or California

State as a whole. It is common for one part of the country to experience a severe economic recession while areas farther away thrive economically.

I looked for out-of-state properties, and I was determined to overcome my reservations about being an out-of-state landlord. I had always questioned why one would buy a house in a faraway place and allow tenants to occupy it. My thinking was that as an out-of-state landlord, I would have no idea of how the house was being taken care of. Having a house close by where I lived allowed me to drive by occasionally and see the outside of the house and at least have some peace of mind if I didn't see any damage on the exterior. I would contend that if the outside looked good, then the inside of the house was also well taken care of. In the end, after some time, I was completely okay, trusting that other people could live in a house and take care of it. The advantages of having all my investments in different areas were many and would mitigate the risks I would face if the economy of Riverside went into recession, resulting in people losing jobs and not being able to rent my houses.

Buying out-of-state properties meant relying heavily on data, be it economic data, demographic data, home sales data, data on schools, crime data, and a lot more. I was amazed to see how much data was out there. The trick was to collect data that applied to the field of research I was focused on and interpret it to achieve my desired end. Reputable firms and organizations publish data periodically that a real estate investor can mine and make an informed investment decision. Firms like the Kiplinger, National Association of Realtors and its state affiliates, Smart Money Magazine, the Census Bureau,

Federal Housing Finance Agency (FHFA), the defunct Office of Federal Housing Enterprise Oversight (OFHEO), Forbes Magazine, and many others released periodic data on real estate. The list of publications containing useful data on various places in the USA is endless.

For the areas I wanted to invest in, I gathered information on crime, cost of living, salaries, schools, quality of life, and favorability to retirees. I found plenty of data comparing and ranking different areas on things like the best places to retire, top-performing metropolitan areas, best places to raise a family, best places for real estate investors, metro areas with the greatest population growth, and cities with the highest home price appreciation.

After I went over the various information packages, I shortlisted cities that had the highest ranking in the following areas:

- Fastest Population Growth,
- Cities With Low Vacancy Rates,
- Fastest Home Price Appreciation Over The Past Ten Years,
- High Level Of Education,
- High Median Incomes,
- High In-Migration Of The Population 35 Years And Over,
- The Fastest Penetration Of The Internet,
- Cities With A Business-Friendly Atmosphere,
- Big College Population,

- Cities Ranked As Best For Real Estate Investors.

I also researched information on areas attracting new investments by national chains like McDonald's, Kentucky Fried Chicken, Starbucks, Lowes, and Home Depot. I knew that those stores do extensive research regarding the economic health of a city before they decide to locate their stores in those areas. I decided to follow those chains in cities where they were locating their new stores. If they had the confidence to spend huge sums of money to open a store in a city, then their economic data showed that the city was on a solid economic foundation.

I looked for properties in Tallahassee, Florida. The areas showed strong economic activity with a large college population and the seat of the state's capital. The city attracted professional, well-educated people working for the state government and the university who would be interested in renting. I had the Florida coastal areas in mind as a backup if I had found some good properties to buy at a reasonably low price to generate positive cash flow. The second area I chose was Dallas-Fort Worth. The metro area was fast growing and attracting people who moved there to take advantage of cheap housing and a strong job market.

I had narrowed down the focus areas, so it was time to decide whether to buy a new home or one that had been lived in previously. Each type of purchase has advantages and disadvantages. The new homes fetched higher rents, were likely to attract more prospective renters, and had state-of-the-art appliances and new construction methods. They were favorites for renters looking to save money on utilities because they were more energy efficient.

I made it a point to avoid the downsides that come with buying a newly constructed house. In many cases, new homes don't have landscaping, which means that as a new owner, you must pay for the installation of landscapes and other things like a concrete patio and patio cover. New homes also rarely have window coverings, which results in spending money to make the house livable. I experienced both situations with the homes I bought in Riverside, California. I had to install landscaping and pay for the installation of concrete patios and window coverings myself.

As I discussed earlier, to save money on landscaping, I had to design and install the irrigation system and the landscaping myself as sweat equity. I bought all the pipes, trees, shrubs, and sod and rented a trenching machine to dig the irrigation trenches. I felt confident that I had done my homework and looked at all the data that I had available in choosing the areas to invest in. I already owned two rental properties in California. It was time to buy out-of-state.

By then, I had staggered my purchases for over two years. Waiting up to two years allowed me to feel financially comfortable after incorporating the new purchase into my finances. It was enough time to figure out if the rental added to the portfolio required me to adjust my finances to avoid strain and accommodate any unforeseen expenditures. It also allowed me to replenish my reserve funds which at times were drawn down to make the purchases possible.

Another rule I had set up for myself was not to buy more than two rental properties in the same state. I had reached that limit in California, and I did not want to violate my own rule. I attended sales presentations by sales representatives from Florida and Texas who pitched their new homes in subdivisions that were under construction. I plowed through many pages of economic reports from those states and researched on the internet to gather data on schools, demographics, and trends in each area. I looked at every detail I knew could affect a buyer's decision: the crime levels, distances from schools, the policies that affected school attendance, and more.

Within the Dallas-Fort Worth area, I settled on a house in a subdivision in the City of DeSoto, a city bordering Dallas. The subdivision developer was using it as a model, winding down sales of homes in the subdivision. All the newly constructed homes had been sold. The location I chose had all the right indicators that I was looking for. The Dallas-Fort Worth area was economically vibrant, with a growing population and home values increasing at an impressive rate.

The data from 2006 and the early part of 2007 showed that the area experienced a double-digit rate of growth in home values. The home was close to downtown Dallas, a location with plenty of good-paying jobs. DeSoto also had good transportation routes leading into Dallas City Center. That meant that even if jobs in DeSoto City ran scarce, there was easy access to the jobs in Dallas. The rental home could attract people who worked in downtown Dallas.

The home itself was relatively cheap compared to California homes. Whereas similar homes in California were selling for close to half a million dollars, the homes in DeSoto were selling for between $150,000 and $200,000. I was careful not to be blinded by the fact that I was used to prices in California, which are higher, and looking at prices in Texas being low but higher compared to sales in the area.

It is common for buyers in high-priced areas like California to overpay for homes in lower-priced states because they consider the price quoted to them in the low-priced state to be a bargain. They end up being overcharged for their purchase. Realtors believed that people from California paid more for homes than the people from the locality because Californians were used to seeing high prices for homes.

As an out-of-state buyer, I took steps to guard against paying too much for the property.

- I talked to other people who had recently bought in the area. Most members of the local real estate investment club were willing to share their experiences and assessments of buying their properties.
- I kept watch on the state of real estate activities in the areas I was interested in to see the number of properties for sale that had price reductions. Such information is available on websites like Zillow. I knew that if there were price reductions, it would have been a sign that the properties in the area were overpriced.
- Also, a quick calculation of the income-to-price ratio can shed light on whether the prices at which the properties are sold are too high. A high price-to-median income ratio of

an area suggests overpriced properties. Income information can be obtained from the US Census Bureau website.

- I also knew that during the loan application, the lender would check to ensure that they were not writing a loan on a property whose value was less than similar properties in the area. If the lender is only willing to fund an amount less than the price you offered, that is an indication that you are paying too much.

Once I decided on the subdivision to buy into, I went on the internet and looked at the neighborhood and street views, thanks to Google. I saw how the neighborhood homes looked and how well they were kept. I also spoke to people in my real estate investment club who had bought homes in the subdivision, and they spoke highly of the area.

One weekend, the club invited sales representatives from different states to give presentations on house products. It was at that afternoon sales event that I finally decided to buy. It was after I attended many sales presentations by Dallas-Fort Worth sales agents. Signing the purchase agreement, I was confident that since it was a new construction, the home would not have major construction defects. I knew that the city Building Department had thoroughly inspected the home before issuing a certificate of occupancy. I was working at the City of Riverside and inspected newly built homes as part of my job. So, I had a good understanding of how the inspection process worked and what national standards had to be met before people were allowed to occupy a home. The chances of ending up spending money repairing major structural, electrical, or plumbing systems were low.

I signed the purchase agreement with the sales lady on a Saturday afternoon, and I wrote a check to hold the house. I had been pre-approved by a lender, which made the process even quicker because I did not have to wait to be approved for a loan. The model home I bought had landscaping already installed in addition to the window coverings. The home builder had opted to rent out the home and had already found a tenant. The broker asked me if I wanted to keep the tenant that the builder had found, and I agreed to keep him, and the rental price set by the developer. That worked in my favor, and as soon as I closed escrow on the house, the tenant was ready to move in.

But before the closing, there were things I had to take care of, like an inspection by my hired inspector. I did not want to rely on what the broker told me about the house as the total truth. I needed to get an independent professional opinion to ensure that everything was perfect. The inspector put together an inspection report, and the house passed in every category. There were no red flags raised, all systems worked all right, all the appliances worked as they were supposed to, and nothing in the yard was of concern. I had found a property manager to manage the newly acquired rental. After signing the management agreement, the manager moved the tenant into the house and collected the rent and the deposit.

## Florida Rental

Unlike other rentals where I had to wait two years before I bought another, soon after I bought the Desoto house, I started looking for a fourth rental. I had found one in Texas, so I looked to buy one in Florida. I have talked about why I chose Tallahassee as the city in which to invest.

I used the same due diligence techniques I used for the DeSoto house to choose a house in Florida. I attended several presentations by realtors from Tallahassee and collected numerous publications about real estate in the city. The house I chose met many of the criteria I was looking for in a rental property. Other Florida cities had good homes; however, Tallahassee, with its seat as the state capital and the university with a big staff and student population, stood out against the rest.

I signed the purchase contract three months after I had bought the DeSoto house; I went against my rule of waiting two years before adding a rental to my portfolio. The property had been discounted, and that played a major role in my decision not to wait. The loan was processed quickly, and within about two weeks, I had approval from the bank.

I had to have the house inspected by a licensed inspector, so I had to find and hire one. As before, I relied on the internet and referrals by club members to find one. The inspection report did not identify any defects; it was a new construction, and the City of Tallahassee building inspector had just issued a certificate of occupancy. Still, I hired my inspector because I did not want the city inspectors' findings to be the only document I relied on. The second inspection report gave me peace of mind.

I received mortgage papers in the mail delivered by United Parcel Services for me to notarize. The papers came from an attorney's office. It was the second out-state property I had to sign closing documents delivered by mail, the first one being the DeSoto, Texas property. The signing instructions were similar in both cases. I presented my identification document to the notary, in this case, a driver's license, and I signed a pile of documents. The signing itself took close to half an hour, after which I immediately put the executed documents in a United Parcel Services envelope and sent them back to Florida. The recording of the documents with the county office in Tallahassee followed.

After I took possession of the property, my next step was to look for a property manager. I used a manager who worked closely with the Marshall Reddick Real Estate Network. The property manager had good recommendations from club members who had hired her prior. The next step was to arrange to have the house keys, garage door openers, and other items picked up by the property manager from the seller. The manager found a renter within a short time, and he was an employee of the nearby Florida State University. The university provided a large pool of renters, which was one of the reasons I picked the area for my investment.

The company managed the property for two years and they decided they did not want to manage it anymore, so I had to look for a new property manager. This time, I did not use managers recommended by the Marshall Reddick Real Estate Network; instead, I searched online to find managers managing properties in the neighborhood. I checked and verified their credentials on the state website that registers property managers. I picked one that had the highest rating by landlords and prior tenants. The company was owned by a woman who explained to me that she had been managing rentals in the Tallahassee area for over twenty years. She agreed to manage my property for the same fee as the prior manager. She managed the property very well and I was satisfied with her services; I had no complaints about her service. She always collected rents on time and took care of the rentals.

# Chapter 16

## Loan Application Process - My Experience

Successful real estate investing involves borrowing money to build wealth. Investors leverage other people's money to finance purchases, which allows them to control the asset while putting little of their money into the property. For that reason, the training classes and seminars I attended placed a great emphasis on the loan application process. Presenters from many lending institutions appeared before the classes to explain and sell their loan products to the attendees.

The first time I went through a loan application was at the end of 1991, when I bought my very first residence. That was before I had attended any of the classes and seminars offered at the Marshall Reddick Real Estate Network. The knowledge I had at that time was what I learned in college class in graduate school.

When I signed the purchase agreement, I had little knowledge of what was to follow after I put in my loan application. The purchase involved a lot of money, and I had signed and committed to buy the property and pay off the loan in 30 years. In the back of my mind, I was asking myself what would happen to me if I failed to qualify for the loan. Was I going to be stuck with a requirement to pay for the property I signed for? After carefully reading the purchase agreement, I noticed that there was a clause saying that the fulfillment of the agreement depended on getting approved for a loan, and without securing a mortgage, I could back out of the deal without penalty.

The loan application process was not much different every time I applied to buy a property. The loan seminars I attended gave me a deeper insight into what to expect, and the process was not as intimidating as when I applied the first time. When I got to buy my second house, I was aware of the hurdles I had to jump over to get a loan.

One information nugget I got from the seminars was to be aware of lenders promoting their loan products. There were lenders or their representatives who would advertise a loan product but only to turn around and switch to sell you something very different. They would bait you in the loan application, and as you proceed through the process, they would switch and try to approve you for a loan that is completely different from the one you started with. That would come at a stage very late in the process and you would be left with no time to look for another lender before the day of closing escrow.

But how would I know which lender plays the bait-and-switch game? I talked to people in the club who were buying properties about which lenders they were using. They knew which lenders stood by their promises as to the loan they would approve me for. Being a member of the investment club helped me to weed out lenders that were bent on taking advantage of borrowers.

The developers I bought my homes from had preferred lenders that they worked with and always encouraged me to use those lenders. I decided to shop around for other lenders to compare loan products. There were advantages in using the developer's preferred lender. One of them was that the application process was smooth, and there was greater coordination between the sales office and the loan officer. The lender and the developer had a close working relationship, and issues that came up during the process were discussed and resolved quickly.

With every property I bought, before starting the loan application process, I would check my credit to ensure that there were no issues that would prevent me from getting approved or getting a good interest rate. I got copies of my three credit reports from Experian, Equifax, and TransUnion credit reporting agencies. I reviewed the reports, and I came up with ways of raising my credit score. There were times when I paid off debt or paid down the balances to raise my scores. Just paying down some debts, especially credit cards, improved my Fair Isaac Corporation (FICO) score and led to a lower interest rate.

The loan application process always began once I entered the sales office and indicated that I wanted to buy a home in a subdivision. The sales representative would show me the available home sites and the type of homes that were to be built on the sites. As soon as I picked a site I wanted to buy, the sales representative would send me to the loan officer to talk about the amount of money needed to buy the house and discuss my income and expenses. I would tell the financial representative about my job, my total monthly income, and how long I had been at the job. I would disclose the debts that I had, the monthly payments and any other financial obligations that I had that may not have appeared in the credit report.

I found out that walking in with a copy of my credit report was always very beneficial because we would discuss my financial situation with hard data in front of us instead of using speculations. It was not the official credit report, but I knew that if they pulled my report, the information would be the same in the reports. The loan officer would enter my information into the computer and tell me if I qualified for the home I wanted to buy. The pre-qualification gave me the monthly loan payment and the amount of money I needed for closing costs. I then knew whether the new purchase would fit into my finances.

Once I was prequalified for the home, I would write a check to the developer, usually ranging between three thousand and ten thousand dollars, to hold the site I picked and take it off the market. That meant that the site would not be sold to any other person as my loan application was being processed for approval, and the house was being constructed.

I always made sure that the purchase agreement I signed with the developer had a contingency clause that if, for some unknown reason, my loan application was not approved, I would get my deposit money back in full. On the other hand, if I unilaterally canceled the purchase, I would lose the deposit. At no time did I lose my deposit because I never canceled any purchase agreement.

I would sign a loan application form and authorize the lender to pull a copy of my credit report to ascertain my FICO score. There was a time when I submitted two loan applications within a week. I did that so that my credit score would not be negatively affected since the credit reporting bureaus would group those inquiries as a single inquiry. If I had waited for months to pass, it would have appeared as a separate inquiry and lowered my credit score.

In all the instances, before I left the office, I was given a list of things I had to collect and bring back to the loan officer to prove that whatever information I gave them to qualify for the loan was indeed true and I was not making up stories. The list of things to bring back included copies of pay stubs for the past month, two months of bank statements, my W-2s for the previous two years, my tax returns for the past two years, copies of my mortgage statements, copies of my credit card statements and car loans. I would prepare a list of my assets and present it together with the list of my debts and income.

Buying a newly built residence under construction would mean the start of a long wait that sometimes was up to six months for the home to be completed, depending on how far along the construction was at the time I signed the purchase agreement. If I signed it when the construction was at an advanced stage, the wait would be much shorter.

Buying my second primary residence, I waited for months before the house was completed. When I walked into the sales office, the developer had just sold all homes in phase one and had just started selling homes in phase two. I applied for a loan with the developer's preferred lender and with an outside lender. The outside lender gave me a pre-approval letter which I gave to the salesperson but instructed her to continue with processing the application with the preferred lender. That forced the developer and the preferred lender to give me additional incentives to finance the house with their loan. The builder offered to upgrade my floor coverings and to buy down the interest rate by a quarter point. Since I was a member of a real estate investment club, I had the option of applying for a loan from one of the lenders that the club leadership recommended. I did not use them because I bought the primary residence outside of the club.

If I had applied with the club-recommended lenders, the process would have been similar. After filling out an application, I would have been pre-qualified and given a pre-approval letter. I would have used that letter to shop for homes. In subsequent purchases, I used the club-recommended lenders. I bought homes from brokers who made sale presentations at the club meetings. The club salespeople did not have homes in Riverside.

## My Second Rental House

For the second rental in Riverside, I signed the purchase agreement in early 2005. Then, there was a quiet period when I did not hear from the lender or the developer. It was not until the end of August 2005 that I heard from the lender, this time asking me for updated documents to make sure nothing had changed since I was pre-approved for the loan.

I sent in the documents, and at about the same time, the developer's sales office contacted me to inform me that an escrow account had been opened for my loan. I knew then that the time was coming close for me to be a landlord for the second time. The sales office did not ask for any updated documents. Instead, I received a letter from the escrow company stating that an escrow account was opened, and I got an escrow number. The escrow company sent me a questionnaire to fill out and send back. It asked for information about my marital status, my full name, and if I had changed my name any time before. In the following days, I received another call from the lender's office who told me that he would be the person processing my loan and would be working closely with me to see that the process was smooth and fast. He also let me know that he had already been in contact with the escrow company and sent them a list of things he wanted me to send to the escrow officer before closing.

The loan process went smoothly, and the information that I submitted had been successfully verified. Three weeks went by, and an appraisal was ordered to compare the prices of sold homes with the price I had agreed upon in the purchase agreement. I paid for the appraisal, and it was listed as money out of pocket in the closing documents. The loan was sent to the underwriter for a more comprehensive review and verification of the information on my file. No time was specified as to how long it would take before closing the loan, but I knew that it usually would be approximately two weeks. After a week, the loan processor called me to tell me that the loan was approved with minor questions that needed verification, like the duration of the lease agreement I had on my first rental house.

Next was to set a date to sign the closing papers. We agreed on a date and time for when I would walk into the escrow office to close escrow. I had the option of signing the loan papers at my home, but that would have involved me paying for a mobile notary to come to my house. I did not want to pay that money because I needed the money to improve the property I was about to own, like putting landscaping and concrete patios.

Signing loan documents was almost like going through a ritual with established norms that had to be met. The notary directed me to a signing room with formal chairs and an executive-looking desk. She said it was going to be strictly business, and I should not answer phone calls or call anyone. I took my California driver's license out of my wallet and a social security card. A couple of times, the notary looked closely at both and then proceeded to use them to notarize documents.

She came into the room with a stack of papers in two file folders. For thirty minutes, she gave me pages with space for me to sign, and on some documents, she had space to sign. She would explain what each document was about and what its legal implications were regarding the loan and the property. The explanations were done very fast. I had to be very attentive to follow the instructions and explanations. I was buying my third home and was familiar with most of the forms but still, the level of intensity was high. In addition, the real estate seminars I had attended through the months had exposed me to almost all aspects of the home buying process, from searching for properties and choosing an area to invest in through loan application up to closing escrow. I made it a point to scrutinize every form presented to me for signing.

At the end of the process, I walked out of the office with two bulging folders full of duplicate loan documents. The house was finally mine. The escrow officer informed me that it was going to take a couple of days for the loan to be funded. That was how long it was going to take for the money to be transferred from the lender's bank account into the account of the developer. The signing officer mentioned that there are usually no problems that arise after the signing. She just wanted to be very cautious.

Once the money was transferred, the escrow company recorded the title with the Riverside County Recorder's office. The house was mine, and I had become responsible for paying the mortgage on a loan that I was to pay for thirty years. It sounded intimidating having to pay for a loan for that long.

What I came to realize is that in this country, homes are treated as commodities, such as corn, oil, or coffee. People buy those homes not to hold on to them for a lifetime but rather to sell them for a profit once equity builds up. This is different from some other countries, such as where I grew up. When a person buys a house, the individual holds on to that house for life. It gets passed down to survivors as an heirloom when the person dies. It becomes a family house that gets to tie generations together and where they gather occasionally as a family. I did not expect to hold on to the house for generations; I intended to hold it as an investment property to sell it after several years and make a profit.

I bought a California rental to benefit from the high appreciation rates in the state; I was not expecting to have cash flow. The historical trend in the state was for the homes to appreciate at an average appreciation rate of seven percent. I projected that if I held on to the house for ten years, there was a high probability that the value of the house would be double what I paid for it. I understood that California goes through boom-and-bust cycles in home values so if I was going to sell it, I would have to sell it at the peak of the appreciation cycle if I was going to realize that profit. Through attending the real estate seminars, I learned several exit strategies that I figured I could use to make a profit. The first primary house I converted to a rental in 2003 had positive cash flow, and if a need arose, I could have used that cash flow to cover expenses on the second rental.

The strategy was different for the homes I bought in DeSoto, Texas, and Tallahassee, Florida. I bought those two homes for positive cash flow, and I intended to own them as long as there was good cash flow.

# Chapter 17

## Lessons Learned Being A Real Estate Investor

Being too loyal to your employer can be detrimental to your financial independence. We were told that we should go to school, get an education, find a job, and work to collect a check from our employer. I put in long hours, and I got paid every two weeks. What I was not taught in school was that the owner of the business or my employer was in it to make a profit or reap financial benefits.

As an employee, I was secondary when it came to the employers' interests. During our formal education, little emphasis is paid to the power of entrepreneurship in generating wealth. As a result, society tends to value a job more positively than entrepreneurship. In other words, society will hold one in high regard if that individual goes to work every day for an employer. It disregards the effort of someone who spends his day working to build his business. It is not until the business starts to flourish that society recognizes the work of the entrepreneur.

When starting out buying investment properties, I was constantly advised not to waste time attending real estate training. It was always unsolicited advice, and there were people who told me how there was no money in rental properties. They pointed out the problems that come with being a landlord. It wasn't until years had passed that those same individuals realized that my properties were valuable and brought in cash flow every month.

Employer loyalty, in many ways, stands in the way of one becoming a millionaire. Most of the millionaires are individuals who spend their hours working on what is in their best financial interests and not the employers' best interests. People who become millionaires working for an employer are mostly top executives at companies that bring in hundreds of millions of dollars every year. Companies that are listed and trading on Wall Street. The problem, though, is that there are not many companies of that stature, and the chances of landing an executive job at those companies are very low. On the other hand, there are many millionaires who got wealthy by working or investing for themselves. It is estimated that over 75% of millionaires built their wealth by investing in real estate, many of them passively. The estimates further show that over half of the accredited investors and high net-worth individuals invest in real estate passively through private partnerships, syndications, private note lending, and private funds.

So how do you exit the rat run when you are starting out and with no money to pay the bills and daily living expenses? The model used by many self-made millionaires who start out as W-2 workers involves dedicating their free time away from their jobs to working for themselves. Start with a hybrid setup whereby you spend time working for your employer and taking time to work on your entrepreneurial projects or investments. Once you reach a point where you can pay your bills with income from your investments or business, it is time to quit your job and start spending more time working for yourself.

I reached a point during my working years when the money I could get as passive income from my rental homes and my pension income was enough to pay for my expenses. I could spend all my time working on my investments in real estate and stocks without giving my valuable time to the employer. I calculated that if I stayed on my job, I would be undervaluing my skills to build wealth. I had acquired skills to work for myself by then, and for any hours I spent working for the employer, I was underpaid. In college, I was introduced to how real estate was financed and developed in the United States. By attending weekend and evening classes and real estate club meetings, I learned how to implement real estate investment strategies.

## Delegating Duties Vs Do-It-Yourself

I was to spend all my time working on my investments, and I had to decide which tasks I would do myself and which ones I would pass on to other people. Deciding which duties to delegate is vital in building wealth.

I realized that money can be compared to a flowing river. The longer the distance the river flows, the less water will remain when it reaches its tributary, assuming no additional water is added along the way. Water is lost along the way. When it comes to money, if several people handle it before it gets to you, it will be less. Whenever possible, and if it adds to your financial bottom line, it becomes important to eliminate the middleman and deal directly with the primary source of the money.

There are times, though, when paying for someone else's service yields greater financial benefits than spending time doing the task. In such instances, the money lost going from one person to another is regained and with bigger rewards. Even though I could have managed my California rental homes, I hired a property manager to manage my rental properties so that I could use that time working at my job, learn more about real estate, and acquire more properties. To be successful in real estate, one needs to learn to establish a balance between a hands-on approach to a problem and delegating to someone else to accomplish the task. It becomes important to delegate if the task will take your valuable time that could be better used bringing more value to the investments.

## Negative Talk And Being Underestimated Or Under-Valued

Negative talk from people around you can bring self-doubt and may hinder the ability to make investing decisions and to be directly involved in investing. So, when I decided to leave my job and spend time working on my ventures, I evaluated my skills, what I could do, and where I needed to strengthen my knowledge. I was surrounded by negative-talking people who doubted my abilities and predicted doom.

I had learned that it was vitally important for me to know what I could accomplish, and I was determined not to be discouraged by people who barely knew me and my abilities. There was never a shortage of people who wished I would fail to prove their hypothesis. They were not convinced that I could achieve success in real estate and thought I had gone crazy. I stayed focused on achieving my goals, and I was not discouraged or held any self-doubt.

When faced with a situation like mine, it becomes necessary to eliminate people from your inner circle who sound negative about what you do. It becomes important to talk more to people who reinforce your goals and encourage you and stay away from people whose intention is to sow seeds of doubt in your mind. Thanks to the education I had acquired, I never lost focus on my goals.

It is absurd that there are people who still judge other individuals based on their color and national origin. Some of my previous co-workers found it hard to believe that I bought the properties I owned all by myself, properties that were in several states. To those people, that seemed impossible, especially for someone like me, an African immigrant for whom they held low expectations. Their perceptions were that if I owned property, it would be dilapidated in a crime-ridden neighborhood. I encountered a similar experience when I went to a job interview. An interviewer asked me to talk about the properties I owned and how I was able to buy them. I talked about how I educated myself about real estate and used that knowledge to acquire the properties. The interviewing gentleman did not believe what I told him. He downplayed my knowledge of real estate and the accomplishments I listed on my resume.

Those negative comments were meant to make me feel like I was less of a person and that I could not accomplish anything major because I was born in a region of the world that, to them, was poor. To those individuals, I always said that a person's place of birth had nothing to do with what becomes of that person when they grow up. My counterargument to them was always like this:

"If you think you were born in an advanced area and therefore much better than me in all ways, then what happened to you that I am much better off than you investing? I am doing better than you are in many areas."

To drive my point home, I would make a football analogy. I let them know that by their argument, they were implying that they started playing the game way before I showed up to play. I showed up in the third quarter to start playing. At the end of the game, I was beating them by 100 points. I would argue that if I was playing against someone who had a late start in the game and that opponent was beating me badly, that was not something to be proud of. It would signify my major weakness and a failure in life for someone who had an early start. Because of that failure in life, I would not spend my lifetime putting my birthplace, which was by accident since I had nothing to do with it, as the proudest thing in my life. And therefore, it would not be the only thing I talk about to lift me up.

I always told them that I had more respect for someone who worked from the bottom and achieved something big than a person who had more opportunities and was only able to achieve little with those opportunities.

## Life Sacrifices To Buy Real Estate

To buy my investment properties, I had to make a lot of life sacrifices. I was criticized for not taking vacations or attending social gatherings during my off-work hours. My vacations were arranged so that they coincided with a project on my property that I had to work on and needed completion. Those projects included installing an irrigation system and laying sod in a front, rear, or side yard. I also used vacation time to go and look for new investment opportunities.

To a few individuals, I was called a workaholic for not spending much time vacationing, taking cruises, or touring Europe and Africa. I also heard some harsh comments that I was not up to the challenge of arranging a vacation. I looked at this issue of not taking expensive vacations very differently. First, I took great joy in what I did during my time off from work and got a lot of satisfaction out of it. Every time I felt like I accomplished something big during that time. Real estate gave me stress relief that was equivalent to being on a relaxing vacation. I would not have substituted that sense of accomplishment and joy for anything else. It helped show my skeptics and people who put me down for either being born in a poor region of the world or not being in a top position at work that I could start and accomplish something that many millions of people could not.

I built a million-dollar-plus investment portfolio from nothing and all that by myself. That gave me a better sense of accomplishment than getting on a cruise ship and returning to my job after a week. True, it would have been more fun to talk about a vacation I took when I returned to the office. However, it wouldn't have given me the same sense of accomplishment and satisfaction as I got working on my properties during my time off work.

## A Sense Of Accomplishment

Different people indeed set different goals in life, and therefore, life accomplishment means different things to different individuals. I have encountered people who set their goals low and thus felt a sense of accomplishment and satisfaction after achieving little things. This was true regardless of a person's background. I consider accomplishment as being able to do what few other people in society have been able to do.

I have seen some immigrants whose discussion of whether they have been able to succeed in this country revolves around whether they were able to travel back to their country of origin to visit. Hence, an immigrant from Africa would consider it an accomplishment if he were able to spend $2,500 to travel back home. That would give them a sense of life achievement and satisfaction. That is an example of setting goals too low.

While building my investments, I looked at things differently. My goals were bigger and a lot costlier than buying an air ticket to travel back to my country of origin. I spent money on real estate education and saving for the downpayment for the homes. So being criticized that I never traveled much or never held lavish parties didn't bother me. I always felt a sense of accomplishment and joy in that I had been able to acquire investment properties. From statistics, I knew that many millions of people, including my critics, had not been able to acquire investment properties.

While I was saving money for the investments, I was at the same time putting my children through school. They got college degrees, and that is another thing that I have always looked at as a personal accomplishment. There are many people I used to speak to, including my coworkers, who would say that they had no one in their family who had a college degree. Here I was, someone who came to this country with nothing, with children who had graduated from college and were holding professional jobs. That gave a soothing feeling to the disappointments I experienced in a workplace where I felt discriminated against.

There are people who treated me differently who did not have children with college degrees. Their discussion would be about how their son or daughter couldn't make it into college or how they dropped out of high school. I did not want to judge them on their parenting skills, but I felt like I accomplished something they were not able to do: preparing my children for success in life. They treated me differently, but they had no power to hold me down; I had the determination to succeed. Their actions fueled the fire inside me to succeed.

Looking back and seeing that I was able to accomplish more than those who treated me differently is a source of joy in my soul. That was proof that racism, xenophobia, culturalism, or other types of discrimination had boundaries on what they accomplish to affect one's success. One must know their skills and strengths and not be dissuaded that they can't do what they want to do.

# Chapter 18

## Advantages Of Real Estate Investing

Being a real estate investor comes with advantages and there are several reasons why I chose to get into real estate investing. I still held a job when I started being actively involved in real estate. I was passively investing in California, Texas, and Florida real estate and generating rental income while working a regular job. This is one of the many advantages associated with real estate. A real estate investor can be miles away from the investment asset or take a vacation for months and still earn money and build wealth.

It was Warren Buffet, the world-renowned successful investor who said, "If you don't find a way to make money while you sleep, you will work until you die." Indeed, many of the wealthiest people earned their wealth from passive investments. Individuals who became super wealthy without passive investments run big, fortune five-hundred companies and collect large annual bonuses. There are only so many such companies; hence, getting to run any of them is out of reach for many people.

With rental properties, it is possible to spend a whole year sailing the world's oceans and still get rich. All it takes is to acquire the rental property, find a property manager to rent it out, and collect rent every month. The property manager can also take care of the repairs, pay the mortgage, and solve any tenant issues that may arise. At the end of the year, you get to enjoy the appreciation plus rent money left over after paying expenses and mortgage debt.

In addition, real estate has a big advantage over other assets when it comes to hedging against inflation. Every year, prices edge higher on most of the day-to-day items we buy. That eats away at the value of the currency we use to buy those items. At the end of every year, we end up spending more of our money than the previous year to buy the same item. Real estate can be used as a tool to protect against inflation and the depreciation of the currency. Property values have risen over the years due to inflation, so real estate provides returns that are adjusted to the risk we incur. That allows real estate investors to preserve the dollar purchasing power.

Real estate's aspect of value preservation can be compared to gold. Gold holds its value over the years to the point that you can buy the same item for the same amount of gold years apart. If a fancy item cost one ounce of gold twenty-two years ago when gold was four hundred dollars in 2003, that same fancy item will cost $2,830 in early 2025, the price of one ounce of gold in 2025. If you had kept your money in a bank, you would have had to spend an extra $2,430 of your cash to buy that fancy item. Considering the interest paid by banks for those twenty-two years, money kept in banks would not have earned $2,430.

Keeping your money in gold allows you to spend the same amount twenty years later. The same goes for real estate. When overall prices rise in the economy due to inflation, real estate prices will follow in the upward direction. The returns on real estate are risk-adjusted, something you don't find on many other investments. This is true even when you consider the fact that real estate experiences brief periods of price depreciation.

We all need to have a roof over our heads. The demand for housing is never going to disappear, and being a landlord means possessing a basic human need. Because of the ever-present demand and need for housing, over the years, rents have risen in step with inflation. For an investor who took out a fixed mortgage to be repaid over thirty years, the monthly payment remains fixed, but the rental income keeps rising due to inflation and increasing rental demand. That translates to a higher cash flow even when you are not actively involved in managing the asset.

Real estate allows you to use other people's money to build wealth. By leveraging, investors own assets with little or none of their money being tied up in the property. A ten thousand dollar down payment on a rental property can make you an owner of a house whose value may be three times higher than the down payment. You get to collect rental income and, at the same time, enjoy the property's appreciation for a minimal amount of your money tied down in the deal.

Added to that, the tenants pay down your mortgage on the rental unit. The investor uses the rent collected to pay down the mortgage and other expenses. When done right, buying a rental property with positive cash flow, all it takes is effective debt management, and the investor's wealth keeps growing daily. The investor becomes the middleman between the bank that financed the rental and the tenants that pay the mortgage. Money comes from the tenant's hand into the investor's bank account, then passes it on to the lender. How good is that!

Another advantage of owning real estate is the tax benefits realized by deducting the property taxes, insurance, repair costs, and depreciation from the income earned. The Internal Revenue Service allows rental property investors to deduct all those items when filing taxes. Depending on the investor's financial situation and the level of participation in managing the rental property, their annual taxes could be reduced to zero even when the investor is holding down a regular job. Like all matters about taxation, it is always advisable to consult a tax expert to decide which deductions fit your financial situation.

In addition to all the benefits of owning real estate, the icing on the cake is the fact that you can show your friends the assets you own without appearing to be bragging. With other assets, such as brokerage accounts, one has to produce account statements to prove ownership. For real estate, the assets are always in plain view.

# Chapter 19

## Life After Retiring From The City Job

After I retired from my job in 2014, I would get up in the morning at 5:30, the same time I used to get up when I was working. I was actively involved in the stock market, and I held stocks in a trading account that I closely followed. The stock market trading started at 6:30 in the morning, so I had an hour to get my breakfast and be ready by the opening bell. Trading stocks is something I did even when I still held a job. I first opened my trading account while still working, and I could follow my stock positions even while I was at work. I learned how to trade options focusing on low-risk trades that did not pose a great risk of loss to me. The market was open until one o'clock in the afternoon, Monday through Friday, so I had the rest of the afternoon and evening open. I had to find something to keep me busy to fill that time; I never liked being idle.

Growing up, I was used to seeing men out of the house every morning, going to look for money to take care of their families. I never saw men staying home, and that stuck in my mind; it was a cultural thing. I wanted to do the same even though I was getting a pension and rental income every month.

At times, I thought to myself that I was playing into the stereotypes about immigrants from Africa. At the city, some of my fellow employees used to talk about such immigrants they knew who never took vacations, sometimes working several years without an extended vacation. I did not want to fit the stereotype. I heard similar stereotypical comments from employees at the post office while I worked there. People talked about Africans as being hard-working people who were able to buy homes in high-value neighborhoods, drove nice cars, and were able to send their children to expensive private schools. I wanted to have a balance between the time I spent working on my investments and leisure activities.

In the workplace, such stereotypical views occasionally resulted in caustic relationships between Africans and other black employees who claimed that African immigrants were given better assignments. I saw no clear evidence that Africans worked much harder than other black employees. The stereotypes, however, persisted and caused suspicion between the two groups.

The divisions and tension between the two groups worked in favor of the supervisors, who were usually people of other racial categories. That was a classic way to divide and conquer. In a country where initial interaction with an individual and how that interaction takes place is always primarily determined by a person's color, the influence of people of African descent was reduced in the workplace.

I never believed in those stereotypes that were tied to African immigrants. I sure worked hard, only occasionally took long vacations, lived in a high-income part of the city where homes were selling above the median home price in the area, and sent my children through college. I may have achieved all that, but I never thought that the other black people were not hard-working. I saw them work long hours, and I knew in my mind that, in many ways, the odds were stacked against them. Society does not give them many breaks in life.

## Going Back To Work At USPS

After two years of staying and working from home, I decided to look for a part-time job. I was missing the daily interaction with other people in the workplace. I, however, did not want to take on work that would occupy many hours in a day, five days a week. At the same time, I did not feel that I could spend many hours a day in the afternoon just sitting at home doing nothing. I was in good health without major health issues with a high probability that I could live for many years in retirement. I looked at some of my close relatives who were older than me but still lived very active lives.

I come from a family that has several people who have lived past one hundred years. My uncle and three aunts were centenarians. There is a possibility that I inherited some of their longevity genes. Therefore, I could live well into my late eighties or nineties, if not one hundred. I was in my late fifties when I retired, so that would be close to forty years of my life. I also knew that being sedentary could lead to health problems and deterioration of my otherwise healthy life.

I was looking for a job with flexible hours and where I would not work more than three days a week. In addition, I did not want a job where I was going to spend a whole day sitting behind a desk since I held such jobs in my prior working years. I wanted work where I would be moving more than sitting down. Moving would get me to exercise, keep me healthy, and avoid taking medications that normally are taken at an advanced age. I looked online and saw that the United States Postal Service was hiring. The job's schedule was flexible, and I could be off work half of the week. It allowed me to stay active, which kept me healthy while I earned income.

Taking the job also saved over seventeen hundred dollars in monthly health insurance premiums. Unlike many other jobs, I was not required to work thirty hours a week to have health insurance coverage; I only had to be on the payroll regardless of the number of hours worked in a week. There were periods when I did not work at all, but I had health insurance, and I paid minimal premiums out of pocket. The premiums I paid were a lot lower due to the employer's contribution.

When I was in my teenage years, I worked for the East African Posts and Telecommunications Corporation, which was my first real job. Ironically, I worked for the USPS, which would become my last job before I permanently retired.

Working part-time after retirement is very common among people of my generation, the Baby Boomers. It is one of the characteristics that sets my generation apart from earlier generations. Unlike our preceding cohorts, we stayed active in the workforce in old age. The Boomer generation is expected to have a longer life expectancy.

# Chapter 20

# Growing My Portfolio – Other Real Estate Strategies I Used

I decided to invest in real estate and chose to educate myself on the many investment strategies that existed. I studied single-family, multi-family, commercial, office, hotel, warehousing, self-storage, and mobile home park investing. I also investigated real estate investment trusts (REITs). All of these made good investment opportunities; however, I narrowed down my selection to vacant lots, single-family, multi-family, and self-storage facility investing. Once I made that decision, I began focusing on the strategy to use. Those investment categories were well suited to my financial situation and the demands of the job I held at the time. Discussed below are strategies that I used to grow my investment portfolio.

## Vacant Lots

While searching for ways to get started investing in real estate, I was introduced to several strategies, one of which was buying vacant lots. My strategy was to diversify my portfolio in terms of location and types of real estate investments. To do that, I bought vacant lots in different states and held them for appreciation. I paid cash for the lots, and I left open the possibility of developing them with homes if I found it financially feasible. Depending on the area the lots were in, I could build the homes and hold them as rental units.

Having worked with cities and a county, I knew the procedures involved in developing raw land with homes and I was familiar with the loan process. I was looking to get a construction loan, develop the lots, and pay back the loan with rent collected every month. I purchased several vacant lots in different states, choosing locations that were close to recreational lakes and within cities where I anticipated growth to occur based on the population projections.

Some lots were in urban areas, which were suitable for development with single-family residences. Others were in subdivisions further out of the city center but in a direction where development was headed. These were the lots that I intended to hold for a long time. I was willing to hold on to them and wait for the surrounding areas to be developed with homes, offices, and commercial buildings, at which time I would construct a speculation home either to sell or to turn into rental properties. I knew that speculation homes as an investment could be profitable in spite of the higher risks involved.

## Multi-Family Residential Units

For years after I started investing in real estate, I focused on single-family residences and vacant lots without paying much attention to apartments. I continually expanded my knowledge in other areas of real estate investing. I studied investing in apartments, and I eventually invested in apartments, starting as a limited partner. I bought into a 544-unit apartment complex where units needed rehabilitation.

After two years, all the units were renovated. The renovations brought the units to the same standard as other units in the area. The work provided the units with quality appliances, floor coverings, plumbing, and wall painting. With the renovations, demand for the upgraded units went up and the rent rose with the increased demand. With the increased rents, the net operating income increased, and as a result, the sale value of the apartment complex rose. For apartments, the net operating income determines the sale price, unlike single-family residences, where comparable home sales in the nearby area determine the value.

## More About Buying Apartments Through Syndication

During classes and seminars on real estate, I was introduced to apartment investing. Presenters talked about the advantages and disadvantages of investing in apartment units. The advantage of buying multiple family units includes the aggregation and spreading of costs among the units. The cost of exterior repairs to the building, for instance, can be assigned to more than one building or apartment unit as opposed to having just one single-family house carrying all costs. As a landlord with single-family rentals, I pay for building repair expenses on the house, and I use income from that residence to cover the costs. I don't spread the costs among other homes.

There is also the advantage of continuing to bring in income in case one unit becomes vacant. Other renters in the apartment complex continue to pay rent, which helps with paying expenses and the mortgage while one unit is vacant.

Additionally, loans for multiple-family residential units bought through syndication are possible for individuals with average incomes. The investor could locate the apartment for sale and then find a sponsor as a partner who qualifies for the loan.

Generally, loans for apartments are approved based on the financials of the property in question. The apartment complex is evaluated in the loan qualification process. The complex must qualify for the loan, and lenders scrutinize the apartment complex's financials a lot more than the individual borrower's income and expenditure. If you find an apartment with good financials where the income that comes in exceeds the expenses and there is sufficient money left over after paying the mortgage, banks will be willing to lend you money with little regard to your income or credit. The key is knowing what your lender requires regarding cash-on-cash, debt service coverage ratio, average rate of return, and internal rate of return. Many lenders will make the loan if the debt service coverage ratio is equal to or above 1.25, meaning that there is money left over after paying for expenses. They may also want to see a cash-on-cash return of at least 8 percent. Lender loan requirements are not universal, and some lenders ask more than others to make the loan.

Another advantage of investing in multifamily real estate is that you control the value of the asset by increasing the income collected and/or lowering the expenses. Above, I talked about the value of increasing the net operating income of the asset. The increased net operating income raises the value of the apartment building. Similarly, if you can lower the expenses, for example, by improving efficiency in the asset's operation or by collecting miscellaneous incomes, the net operating income increases. All these actions are under the control of the apartment owner. For single-family residences, the value of the house is determined by the comparable sales in the area, something you, as an individual investor, cannot control.

Investing in multi-family units, I started by looking for apartment complexes that were relatively small and located in Southern California. The strategy I intended to use to buy the units was a 1031 Exchange whereby the Internal Revenue Service allows investors to defer paying capital gains taxes if the proceeds of the sale are reinvested in similar but more expensive property. With that approach, I would have sold one of the single-family rental properties to buy the apartments while deferring paying capital gains taxes.

I discussed my plan with my loan broker and other more experienced investors, after which I was convinced that there were other approaches I could use to acquire apartments without selling any of my rental houses. One of those approaches was to get involved by investing as a limited partner. That meant that I had to educate myself more on how syndications operate and what the risks versus rewards were. Like any other investment, it is crucial to evaluate what to expect prior to putting money into an investment. I learned how to underwrite properties to know their fundamental financial aspects like net operating income, capitalization rate, cash-on-cash return, internal rate of return, annual rate of return, and debt service coverage ratio. Knowing those financial parameters allowed me to pick which apartment properties were a better investment.

I chose to invest as a limited partner in an apartment complex that was offered for sale. The general partner was seeking investors with a net worth of over one million dollars. This was meant to meet the Securities and Exchange Commission requirements under Rule 506(c), which was established by the US Securities and Exchange Commission (SEC) under Regulation D of the Securities Act of 1933. The rule allows companies to raise capital from accredited investors.

I contacted two asset verification companies to establish the value of my assets and, thus, my personal net worth so that I could invest in the apartment complex. Once the assets were verified to be over one million dollars, excluding the primary residence, the general partner accepted me as a limited partner, and I became a part owner of a 215-unit apartment building.

## Single-Family Residences Vs Multi Family Residential Investing

By then I had discovered the advantages of investing in apartment units and could make an informed comparison between buying more single-family residences versus acquiring apartment units. One of the many advantages of investing in real estate is the ability to build a nest egg for retirement. Real estate is also a good tool to build a legacy that you can leave behind to children. This can be accomplished by buying single-family residences, multifamily units, or both. Each of these asset types has advantages and disadvantages and as an investor, one must pick which one of them best suits his or her situation.

There is no right or wrong approach to investing in each of these assets. It all depends on each investor's situation and preference.

To start, I chose to invest in single-family residences. It was an easy pivot since I turned my first home into a rental when I bought a bigger house for my family. That house provided the seed money that I used to acquire more rentals as time went by. I took advantage of the benefits that come with buying single-family homes that were not available to a beginner apartment investor, such as qualifying for a loan and a smaller down payment. Apartment lenders want to collect a big down payment, usually at least 25% of the purchase price. On the other hand, lenders for single-family residences can approve a loan with a small down payment, at times as low as 3.5 percent.

Without prior experience in apartment investing, my start in multi-family investing was through syndication by partnering with other investors. Through self-education, I recognized the many advantages that come with apartments. I also knew that if I invested in apartments, it would be easier to raise money to invest through syndication. There are well-established procedures and federal rules that govern raising capital through syndication. I spent time continuing to educate myself on how to raise capital and other aspects of multi-family investing, including underwriting. My goal was to identify a well-structured deal with no less than fifty units that presented me with an opportunity to generate a minimum of 100 dollars of positive cash flow per unit.

## Tax Deeds And Tax Liens:

I invested in tax deeds and tax liens by accessing information on different tax collectors in various states, including Arizona, Florida, Texas, and Kansas. Once I invested my money, the County Tax Collector in the counties I invested in collected the money and sent me a check. In the chapter below, I discuss the processes of how tax deeds and tax liens sales are sold. Most of the work involved in tax deeds and tax lien investing can be done at home over the Internet.

# Chapter 21

# Other Investing Strategies I Considered But Did Not Use

There are numerous real estate investment strategies, and before I settled on buying vacant lots, single-family residential rental homes, tax liens, tax deeds, and apartments, I studied many strategies to figure out which one best suited my situation. I will explain each of them and point out the lessons I learned.

## Sharing Equity In Investment Property

Through the equity share approach, two or more investors combine their finances, expertise, and time to buy property. Ownership in the property is apportioned between the investors according to an agreed-upon formula. Equity share allows investors to get a head start in real estate investing without waiting to overcome obstacles that may hold them back. In times of fast value appreciation, the equity share approach can let you acquire property immediately and not be priced out while you wait to overcome an obstacle, like raising a down-payment.

One investor may have the capital required for the down-payment and the other may have the employment history to qualify for a loan. Or one investor may have the money, while the second investor has the construction skills necessary to renovate the house, thereby saving thousands of dollars that would have been spent on hiring contractors. The combination of skills investors can combine to buy a property through sharing equity is limitless.

Similarly, using the equity share method, one investor can bring the down payment while the other individual brings the closing costs money. Another approach is for one person with a good credit rating to enter into a deal to buy a house with another individual with bad credit but has the money for a down payment and closing costs. The two parties can then sign an agreement spelling out how they will split ownership of the property. It is a good idea to have the equity share agreement reviewed by professionals. To get an idea of how to structure the agreement, one can review such agreements found on several real estate websites. It is, however, important to have an attorney involved in preparing the agreement.

The equity share strategy has allowed many investors to scale their portfolios. Once the home appreciates and/or the debt is paid down, it could be sold, and thereby come up with a down payment for another house. In times when money is cheap, you can buy properties with low interest rates and lock in those low rates and end up saving a lot of money during the hold time. In places like California where home prices appreciate very fast and where there is a possibility of being left out of home ownership, equity share is a great strategy to get into real estate. Over the years, you can pull out your equity from the property and buy a property that you own alone. It makes raising the down payment possible where you would otherwise have been left out of investing.

I have seen a situation where two investors teamed up to buy a home in a city where they both had sons attending college. They bought a four-bedroom house, and their children occupied two bedrooms while the other two bedrooms were rented out. The investors saved on the costs of holding the home since they were collecting rent from the two tenants. They also avoided paying for expensive college dormitories while at the same time building equity in the home. The key is to find an investor with a like mind willing to enter into an equity share arrangement.

As with any other type of investment, there are risks that come with the equity share approach to real estate investing, and those risks must be carefully evaluated. For one, it is important to find an investor with the same investment goals and risk tolerance who will be willing to have their invested money tied up in the house for as long as you are willing. Some people have a low threshold for risk and will want to get out of the investment even with a few signs of trouble. You shouldn't have a partner who would want to sell the property to avoid headaches if, for one month, a tenant was late with rent. Or having an investor who would want to sell the property because a tenant moved out and left the house in terrible shape and needing extensive repairs. You want to invest with someone who realizes that such situations are some of the issues landlords regularly encounter.

Successful Investing is maximizing profits by selling at the right time when you can get the most profit. Selling just because a tenant did some damage to a property will most likely leave you with minimal profits or a loss. There is no easy way to get profits if the property is sold at the wrong time because your partner has different goals or has a low threshold for risk. You must be ready to go through some hard times. Making money in real estate is not a walk in the park, and occasionally, there will be painful financial moments. Think of the job you go to in the morning, Monday to Friday. There are times when you have to go through unpleasant times at work; maybe your boss is giving you a hard time. You don't just get up and quit. You stay on the job, knowing that those times will pass and the situation will get better.

If you take the time to find investors with compatible goals, the combinations of workable equity share partnerships are endless. Your real estate agent can be your equity share partner. Your handyman can be a great equity share partner, especially if you are into buying and rehabilitating properties. You can provide the down payment and qualify for the loan, and the handyman can provide his services by doing all the repairs to rehabilitate the property. The equity share of ownership can be negotiated.

A homeowner who finds himself in a hard financial situation can also be a great equity share partner. You can provide the homeowner with cash to get out of the tough situation, and in return, you share ownership of the property. You must get a detailed and well-crafted legal agreement spelling out your ownership and responsibilities and record a new grant deed with your name. The owner can choose to stay in the house or move out to make the house a rental. With time you may decide to buy out the former owner and take 100% possession of the property.

So why would a homeowner want to co-share to get out of a hard financial situation? The homeowner may want to raise money to diversify his or her investments. By entering into an equity share arrangement, the homeowner avoids going through a loan application process and qualification to get a home equity line of credit or cash-out refinance. The owner saves money by avoiding loan fees, closing costs, and other charges.

A not-so-common equity share partnership, which is possible all the same, involves divorcing couples. Such equity share partnerships are more complicated to put together due to the emotions that rage during the divorce. Having a couple go through the intricacies of putting together an equity share agreement can be complicated.

Finding a compatible investing partner can't be over-emphasized to avoid pitfalls. If you are the partner putting up your income and assets to qualify for the loan, that implies that your credit is on the line should there be missed payments. If you are the partner who brings the cash, you are risking your money and are at a greater loss should the investment fail.

## Buying And Renovating Repossessed Homes

As I was exploring what strategy to use in investing, I investigated buying homes that required repair and renovating them for resale. My intention was to build on the renovation skills I had used to renovate my first owned home while preparing it for renters. The real estate classes I attended introduced this strategy, and I wanted to try it in the real world.

The strategy involves searching for homes that owners or lenders want to sell for various reasons and buying them at a discount below the median price in the location. After taking possession of the house, the investor puts together a team of contractors to do the renovation. In a typical renovation process, the house is then put back on the market for sale.

To realize a profit from the sale of the house, a key factor is that the investor has to find sellers that are willing to sell at less than the value of similar homes. These are sellers who are experiencing some form of hardship and are eager to get rid of the house. The homes are usually not in the best form and require a considerable amount of work to upgrade them to compete with comparable homes for sale. The investor gets the most benefits if they buy homes located in nice neighborhoods with good schools and preferably only needing cosmetic repairs.

Flipping homes comes with greater risks than the buy-and-hold strategy. The strategy requires that you make no major mistakes since there is no benefit of time to correct the errors. Among the key aspects of employing this strategy is the need to ensure that you acquire a property at a discount to be able to sell it at a profit after all the repairs are completed.

To put it differently, the after-repair value of the flip must make financial sense. The after-repair value is arrived at by adding the price paid for the property, the cost of the repairs, and the cost of holding the property. Holding costs generally include expenditures like property taxes, HOA dues, insurance, interest on the loan, utilities, and advertising. Most flips are financed by private money loans with the intention to refinance into a conventional or agency loan after the renovations are completed. Those loans generally require a loan-to-value ratio of at least 75 percent. To be able to refinance out of the private money loan, therefore, requires that the value of the property be more than the total cost of property acquisition, repairs, and holding costs by at least 75 percent.

For instance, if you buy a distressed property for $200,000 and spend $60,000 on repairs and $10,000 on holding costs, your after-repair value should be at least $270,000. That is the break-even amount. To be able to refinance into a conventional loan or agency loan, the appraised value of the house has to be $360,000, which represents the 75% loan-to-value.

When engaging in this strategy, it is advisable to consult a tax professional for information on how the tax code will tax the profits. If the house is bought and sold in less than a year, the Internal Revenue Service will require you to pay short-term capital gain taxes, which are based on your tax bracket. This could be high, reaching 30 percentage points depending on your annual income.

If you bought the house, renovated it, and sold it after one year, the profits are long-term capital gains and taxed at a lower rate, ranging from no taxes on the profits to 20 percent. The IRS allows investors in the 10 percent or lower tax bracket to pay no taxes on capital gains. Many of the investors I have seen fall within the 22-percent and 32-percent tax bracket, and they pay a 15-percent tax on the profits realized at the sale of the home. The highest long-term capital gain tax paid on flipped house sales is 20 percent by those investors in the higher tax brackets. So, if you buy the house and can hold on to it for a year, there can be big tax savings.

Savvy investors can apply other methods to reduce or avoid taxes on the capital gains realized. One method is to live in the renovated house for two years out of the five years the investor owns the house by utilizing IRS Section 121 Primary Residence Exclusion. The amount excluded from taxes is $250,000 for a single filer and up to half a million dollars for joint filers.

In addition, the investor can postpone paying taxes by using a 1031 Exchange. This requires using the profits to buy a similar investment property within six months. As in other tax related matters, it is always good to talk to a tax adviser.

I analyzed a hypothetical scenario in which I bought a house, renovated it, lived in it, and sold it after two years. Under that scenario, I would pay no capital gains taxes. Instead, I would look for another fixer-upper to renovate and roll the tax-free profits into the new house. My calculation showed that it was possible to quadruple my net worth in ten years, assuming a California average annual appreciation of seven percent.

After I evaluated the pluses and minuses of renovating and sale of the homes approach and how it would fit into my regular job schedule, in addition to having the responsibility of raising my children, I concluded that it would have been difficult to implement. It would require some substantial sacrifices in the initial years of ownership, which would have meant cutting back on expenditure on children. I was the only source of financial support for the children, who had no help coming from their mother. It would have negatively affected the children's well-being, and it would have been impossible for them to buy school supplies and pay for their extracurricular activities. Those are some of the sacrifices you make as a parent.

## Self-Storage Facility Investing

I investigated and educated myself in investing in self-storage facilities as a way to diversify my investment portfolio. I learned that self-storage facilities are easy to manage, and when there is a turnover in occupancy, the make-ready costs are minimal compared to housing units. The facilities also tend to weather economic downturns much better than other asset types. People who are hard hit by the recession will look to share housing arrangements and store their belongings in storage facilities. In recent years, there has been an increase in demand for self-storage units from both businesses and homeowners and renters.

# Chapter 22

# Commonly Used Strategies For Investing In Real Estate:

## Ways To Get Started

Real estate can make you wealthy if you have the determination and put in the effort to learn and do the work. To become a millionaire investing in real estate, it is important to start by setting goals. Create a vision of where you want to be, which is to join the millionaire club. You can achieve that vision by coming up with a plan that is tailored to your circumstances. To start investing, you do not need to have tens of thousands of dollars. You only need determination, a willingness to learn, and the courage to take the first step.

First, look at the resources or opportunities available to you and evaluate your skills that you can utilize to take advantage of those opportunities. For instance, if you know how to repair or install house floors, that is a skill that you can use to add value to the rental unit. You would not be spending money on hiring a floor installer if you could do it yourself. The more knowledge you have about fixing various things on the house, the more money you will save on repairs and, the more profits you will make when you sell the house. When starting out, every dollar you can save through sweat equity can go a long way in your effort to be successful.

If there is a skills deficit, that is the time to go out and acquire those skills by learning new things. This may involve taking classes, going to seminars, and joining groups where you can interact with people who have the skills you want to acquire. Whatever means are available to you, use them to acquire the necessary skills. Getting started, investing requires capital, and if you can save money through sweat equity, the higher the chances of success.

Once you draw up a plan to achieve your vision, set goals that will enable you to reach it. Goals written down on paper are easier to pursue and achieve than unwritten goals. I broke my goals down into small, achievable, and measurable segments to avoid looking at them as huge obstacles that could not be handled. For each segment of the goals, I identified the tools I could use. You can even show your goals to your friends or family members, but only those who will encourage you to pursue them. Negative talkers have to be avoided, and you may have to eliminate them from a list of friends you discuss your future plans with. That may sound rather harsh or cruel. However, many people who quit pursuing their goals are influenced by negative, discouraging comments they hear from those they communicate with. Those negative comments create doubts in the minds of the investor, who start to doubt their decisions and break their resolve to do whatever they set out to do. I have talked about people who I worked with and who always said that I couldn't be successful in real estate. I had to avoid talking about my vision with them to stay focused on my dreams. Those are steps I took and found helpful on my journey to becoming a real estate investor. I believe they can benefit many individuals who want to be investors.

Like all types of investments, whenever you commit money to an investment, you are taking on some level of risk. To have any gain, you must take on a level of risk. The key is to know how much risk you can afford to take on and balance the risks and the benefits. There are critical decisions that you must make and mistakes that you have to avoid.

Since I became a landlord in 2004, there have been lessons learned and mistakes made. To this date, I have not yet met an investor who says that they have never made mistakes on their journey to success. Mistakes and failures have a way of teaching us lessons and sharpening our skills which leads to making better decisions in the future. Anyone who claims never to have made mistakes is telling us that they do not set and try to achieve goals.

There are many other strategies in real estate investing through which one can make money and become a millionaire. Above, I have talked about the strategies I have used to invest. That doesn't imply that they are the best for every investor; they were good for my situation. Anyone who wants to get involved in investing can try other strategies. I will list strategies that I have come to know and have been used by many investors.

## Buy And Hold

With this strategy, an investor buys a property and holds on to it for many years, sometimes decades, while the debt is paid down and the home appreciates in value. Eventually, the mortgage is paid off, and the property is held free and clear. Using an average appreciation rate of seven percent every year, an investor who can afford to buy five rental homes in their first year of investing for $100,000 each could have a real estate portfolio of over a million dollars in ten years. That portfolio value would be a combination of appreciation and debt pay-down using collected rent.

In California, rents have averaged between 4 and 5 percent growth every year in the past ten years. The wealth built and rental income collected could allow one to retire from their job within ten years of starting their investing journey. Retiring from a nine-to-five job could allow the investor to focus on real estate investing full-time.

Buy and hold has the added advantage of mistakes of the past to self-correct as time passes. If, for instance, you commit an error at the time you buy the asset by overpaying, that error can be corrected by an increase in the value of the asset as years go by. On the other hand, if the time you hold the asset is short, the asset's value will not appreciate enough to overcome the mistake.

## Buy, Renovate, And Sell The Property Or Flipping

This strategy yields better results when the real estate market is vibrant, with strong demand and rising prices. It is one of the riskiest strategies, but it can bring in big profits if successfully done. The process of buying the house, renovating it, and selling it could take between six and eight months. Within the hold period, the market conditions could change. The risk involved with this strategy is that if the market takes a downturn during the renovation, you could lose money by selling the house for less than you invested.

## Buy, Rehabilitate, Rent, Refinance And Repeat

To start off, the investor buys a property that is usually rundown and rehabilitates it to where it is habitable. The rehabilitated property could become a rental or a primary residence of the investor. After owning the house for a while, the investor refinances the loan, sometimes taking out money, and turns the house into a rental house to generate income. The equity pulled out of the rental is used to buy another house that also requires renovation, and the cycle is repeated.

This strategy can also work for investors who want to save on capital gains taxes if they live in the house for at least two years of the five years they own it by using IRS section 121 – exclusion of gain from the sale of primary residence for tax savings.

## Syndication

I have touched upon this strategy above as one I have used to invest in apartment buildings. With syndication, a group of people come together and pool their money with a common goal of investing in real estate. The investors form a legal entity, usually a limited liability company, to buy property. There is always a general partner. That individual acts as the frontman when applying for a loan, looking for and acquiring the property, and running the day-to-day affairs of the company. The other syndicators or limited partners are not actively involved in the acquisition process or overseeing the investment. They are passive investors and may get paid distributions on a regular basis. When the property is sold, they share the profits in accordance with the percentage of ownership. This is a good avenue to get into real estate investing, especially if you have a job that you love and don't want to quit. You participate in the investment passively.

## Real Estate Investment Trusts (Reits)

These may or may not be traded in the same way as stocks on the stock exchange. This strategy allows small-scale investors with limited amounts of money to invest in real estate. Investors pool money together with a chance to invest in apartments, hotels, commercial and office buildings, and many more. The Securities and Exchange Commission regulates REITs, which typically buy already-developed properties. Rarely do they purchase raw land and develop. Publicly traded REITs are listed on the stock exchange, while private REITs are not. The traded REITs sell shares for partial ownership of the properties, like regular company stocks.

## Crowdfunding

This approach uses online platforms to raise money from many investors who sometimes contribute small amounts. The investors buy an asset, and by pooling money together, each investor receives a slice of the asset and gets part of the proceeds if the asset realizes a profit. Similar to REITs, crowdfunding is regulated by the Securities and Exchange Commission.

## Rental Conversion

Many investors get into real estate investing by converting their primary residence into a rental unit. The money they collect from tenants is used to pay the loan and related expenses such as property taxes and repairs. Since 2019, during the COVID-19 pandemic, rents have risen sharply to the extent that some homeowners decided to convert their homes into rentals and become renters themselves if they paid less rent than the money they collected from their tenants.

## Wholesaling

For many investors who lack the capital to start investing, wholesaling is a common way to raise seed money. It involves finding properties for sale, putting them under contract, and then looking for a buyer with money and assigning the contract to them for a fee. After finding and assigning several properties, the investor could raise capital to buy and own real estate.

## Short-Term Rentals

Short-term rental units are a newer category that started to become popular in 2008 with the establishment of Airbnb. This company created an internet platform that allows individuals to rent homes for short periods, sometimes for just a single day. Renting out homes for a short time has proven to be a lucrative strategy, and many investors praise the returns they get on their invested money.

## Debt Snowballing And Debt Avalanche Strategies

Under the debt snowballing approach, the investor acquires several properties with positive cash flow. The positive cash flow is used to pay off one property at a time. The strategy focuses on paying off the smallest mortgage first. Once paid off, the focus turns to paying off the next smallest mortgage, then the next, and so on, until all the properties are held free and clear.

Debt avalanche strategy, on the other hand, focuses on interest rates on the mortgages held. The investor starts by paying off the mortgage with the highest interest rate. The money saved by paying off the first mortgage is then used to pay the loan with the next highest interest rate. The process continues until all the mortgages on properties acquired are paid and they are owned free and clear.

## Tax Liens And Tax Deeds

Counties throughout the USA assess property taxes on real estate that owners must pay periodically. If the taxes are not paid, the County collects the money owed through tax deeds or tax lien sales. Tax lien and tax deed investing do not require large sums of capital to start.

Some states conduct tax deed sales, while others have tax lien sales. Some combine both. The common thread between the two is that the sales take place after the property owner fails to pay delinquent property taxes.

For tax liens, if the property owner fails to pay their property taxes for several years, the county advertises the property. The investor with the highest bid pays the county's delinquent property taxes. The investor then earns interest on the money used to pay off the taxes. The interest paid varies from state to state and can be in the high twenties. Florida tax liens are known to pay some of the highest interest rates. The county treasurer collects the money and then passes it on to the investor.

The original owner is allowed time in which to pay off the delinquent taxes and regain ownership of the property. To do so, however, the county collects the original taxes owed plus the interest earned and passes the money on to the investor. The investor is responsible for payment of subsequent taxes between the time the county sells the tax lien to owner redemption. If the property owner fails to pay the money owed, the investor takes ownership of the property by filing legal papers with the county.

In states that hold tax deed sales, properties with delinquent taxes are advertised, and the highest bidder takes ownership of the property immediately. Some states allow a redemption period during which the delinquent owner can pay the taxes, interest, penalties, and expenses to regain ownership of the property. In other states, the delinquent owner loses the property with no chance of redemption.

## Private Money Lending

Investing in loans is another avenue one can use to invest in real estate. This investing strategy has been around for a long time, with wealthy individuals making loans to real estate borrowers either to finance a first loan on an investment asset or as a second mortgage. Such private loans are commonly used by investors who buy homes and remodel them for resale. They are also used by apartment investors who use them as bridge loans to refurbish apartment units to be able to refinance into a better loan, usually an agency loan by FANNIE, FREDDIE MAC, or HUD.

Private money lending regulations vary from state to state and are less stringent. It is important to find out which laws apply in the states you are lending in. California's usury laws, for instance, require private money lenders to get licensed, and there are net-worth requirements that must be met. The interest on real estate loans tends to be higher than traditional loans, usually double-digit.

There are pros and cons that come with private money lending. So, it is necessary to match the strategy with your overall business plan. In addition to being less regulated, private lending yields higher interest rates. The terms of the loans are also more flexible and require less paperwork. On the other hand, the loans have a higher risk of default and a higher possibility of losing the money lent. For one, the loans tend to be in second position, and therefore, in case of a foreclosure, there is a chance that only the first loan lender recovers their money.

## Acquiring Vacant Land

The cost of vacant land tends to be less than land that is developed in any way. Prior to buying, it is crucial to know the applicable rules regarding the future use of the land. Counties and municipalities have zoning laws that can limit the manner in which the land can be used, which in turn could prohibit the investor from recouping the money. The value of vacant land is greatly influenced by what the land can be used for. If the land is purchased to subdivide into lots that can be developed separately, the investor needs to know restrictions as to the minimum lot size, width, depth, and accessibility. Also important is the need to research the demographics and economic factors in the area. A lot located in an economically vibrant area can be used to generate income by using it for temporary activities, such as Christmas tree sales or Halloween-related events. Maximum profits from vacant land investment are attained if the location of the lot is in the path of development. The value of the lot increases as the surrounding areas develop.

## Developing Vacant Lots

This approach works well when building speculation homes. Vacant land is developed without a prospective buyer at the start of construction and with the hope that once the house is completed, it will be marketed and sold for a profit. One way to finance the construction is by pulling money from properties you already own and avoiding borrowing.

If you cannot self-finance, then you can get a construction loan either from a bank or a hard money lender. Once completed, the house can be rented out, or it could be sold for cash to recoup the money invested and pay back the loan.

Another approach is to share equity with another investor if you own the lot free and clear. You, as the owner of the vacant lot, can offer the market value of the lot as your contribution to the partnership while the other partner brings cash as their contribution toward the joint venture. The money is used to develop the lot, and after the property is sold, profits are shared as agreed.

A suitable strategy is always based on an investor's goals and circumstances. A strategy that may be suitable for one investor could be disastrous to another. It is always better to know your financial strengths and weaknesses before you commit money to acquiring property. A lot of homework is needed; however, this does not mean that it is impossible to get started in real estate investing. The good thing about real estate is that all the necessary work can be done even when you still hold a regular W-2 job. You don't need to put in eight hours every day to start your investing successfully. Most of the work can be done on your computer, tablet, or cellphone. You could put in as little as five hours a week and still succeed. This is work that you can do over the weekend or after work. Take time to do a financial evaluation and then consider the investing strategies available to you and pick one that suits you.

I have discussed how I started as a real estate investor and how I spent time assessing what I could do to start investing, knowing that I needed to keep my job. Buying and holding homes for a long time, buying vacant land, syndication, and tax deed investing turned out to be my better match. House flipping was one of the strategies I seriously considered. In the end, I concluded that it would not suit me at that time. I had to hold down a regular job to support my family. The job was one of the three pillars I used to build wealth, in addition to stocks and real estate. Those three pillars had to complement each other.

There are common factors that run through all of the strategies that will increase the chances of your success as a real estate investor. First, you need to get started by acquiring the necessary knowledge. You don't have to be an expert, but you have to educate yourself with sufficient knowledge before you start. Once you have done that, it is time to buy property. You could start by buying just one property. That first property will teach you a lot, and many of the questions and uncertainties that you have in your mind will start to dissipate. I would not advise starting with multiple rental units, even if you may be financially able to afford them. Gradual learning and correcting mistakes made with your first purchase can be the best learning tool available to you.

You should keep observing and learning from experts or more experienced individuals. The key here is to find someone who has implemented the strategy you have picked and shadow them to learn the inside tricks. As I said earlier, one of the reasons investors fail is that they surround themselves with negative people who feed them negative information that is sometimes not true. Watching television news stories by people who refer to themselves as experts but spread negative information instead can lead to your failure as an investor. You have to be judicious. You may, therefore, have to avoid friends and media outlets that are negative and may lead you to start doubting your decision to invest. Find and attend local club meetings and online educational webinars and groups where you will interact with investors of like minds who will reinforce your desire to be successful. In quorums like those, you will find people who share their experiences and lessons learned. Such knowledge can save you money and time. Minimizing interactions with negative people or news outlets and online groups is necessary to reach your goals.

To a beginner investor, starting with properties with positive cash flow is important if you don't have a large pot of reserve funds or much discretionary income. Avoid acquiring properties that don't financially self-sustain. For people who live in states where real estate is expensive, finding such positive cash-flowing properties will require that you buy out-of-state.

Due diligence is another vital aspect not to ignore if you are going to succeed. Thoroughly research the area you want to invest in, investigating all aspects of the area and the property. Nothing causes loss of money faster than buying a property with so many problems that drain your funds once you acquire it or buying property in an undesirable area that makes it unrentable.

To avoid extreme risk exposure, invest in different regions and in different asset classes. Look to buy properties in areas that have different demographics and economic characteristics. If all your investments are in one area and that area experiences an economic downturn, you will be hit hard financially. You could end up having several properties that stay vacant for a long time because people lost their jobs. As you get more experienced, it is also a good idea to diversify the type of properties you invest in. If you own several single-family residences, invest in apartments, self-storage, or mobile home parks, for example.

For one to succeed in real estate, investing does not have to seem like a chore; rather, it should be something you enjoy doing even when times are hard. As long as you stay invested in your properties for a long time, you are going to run into hard, challenging times. If you consider real estate to be a chore, as soon as the hard times strike, you are likely to look for an exit and most probably take a big loss. If real estate investing is something you do out of love, you can easily ride out the hard times, and when you get to the other side, you are likely to enjoy good profits.

Many investors fail to start investing in real estate because they think they have to know everything and all the information they are presented with. They spend a lot of time analyzing investment opportunities that come their way and never start investing. My advice in this situation is that you need to pick a strategy you want to use for investing. Once you pick the strategy, know enough to avoid making disastrous errors and go out there and start investing. As you spend time in the game, the better investor you become. Don't be afraid of making mistakes. They are your best teacher.

# Chapter 23

## Implement Your Chosen Strategy: Picking An Area To Invest

By now, you have decided that you are going to be a real estate investor and have also chosen what investing strategy to use. The next task is to search and find a region of the country to invest in. In the earlier chapters, I discussed how I started my real estate investing journey and how I chose to buy my rental homes in the neighborhood I lived in and knew well. When searching for areas to invest in, I suggest that you start by looking close to home. If you don't find properties or neighborhoods that meet your criteria, then you can search in areas farther away. To have a wider selection, you can extend the search area to neighborhoods within a one-hour driving distance from your home.

If you search and buy locally, you have many advantages, including knowledge of the market. You know what the conditions of the real estate market are like, including the strength of the rental market. It is also easy to build a team to work with while building your portfolio. You can get referrals from friends and relatives, unlike working in faraway places where such help may not be readily available.

There will be times when you can't find properties to buy in your local area and are forced to buy out-of-state. A case in point is California, where homes are expensive and where getting positive cash-flowing rentals is almost impossible within the first years of ownership. It takes time to get rental properties to yield positive cash flow. Sometimes, this is achieved through rising rents or refinancing the mortgage to lower the monthly payment. You are therefore left with the one alternative, which is to look in faraway places to find rentals that can cash flow positively.

To make the search less cumbersome, you can start with an area covering an entire US Census Bureau's Statistical Metropolitan Area (SMA). SMAs have economic and demographic data that can guide you to which areas have a favorable investing environment. The US Census Bureau reports information by SMAs, and looking at that information, you can see which areas of the country contain the demographic and economic characteristics that you are looking for in an investment area. You can quickly identify which regions of the country are expanding or contracting economically. You then narrow your research to focus on smaller areas within the SMA, like counties or cities. Look for the following in an area:

## Growing Population And Households

Choose areas with a growing population where household formation is on the upswing. A growing population means a large pool of renters to rent to and a higher rental demand. Likewise, household formation increases demand for rentals as young people leave their parent's homes or get married to establish a family, start having children, and start looking for places to raise their families.

A growing population also attracts businesses and government services, which create new jobs. Businesses set up shop to serve the growing number of people looking for goods and services. New businesses generate more jobs and more people with income looking for a place to rent.

## Quality Of Schools

Schools play a vital role in deciding where renters and home buyers choose to live. As an investor, you will get better tenants and get your unit rented faster if it is in an area with good-performing schools. It is an established fact that the quality of schools greatly affects the value of a rental unit and its appeal to potential renters. Some of the characteristics to look for are the school's academic performance on standardized tests, the school's graduation rates, and recognition of excellence in academic fields. Other positive aspects to consider are low teacher-to-student ratio, access to educational resources, availability of extracurricular programs, parental involvement, and staff and student diversity and inclusion. All these factors contribute to a better quality of schools, which translates into higher property values and rental desirability.

## Positive Rate Of Return

The need to invest in an area where you can get a positive rate of return can't be over-emphasized. This decision can be highly individualized since some investors can withstand a low rate of return initially to benefit from future property appreciation or rent growth. I bought a new rental home in California, and I was nowhere close to positive returns on my investment. I bought the house solely for appreciation and after I had confirmed that I had sufficient reserves and income to cover the rent shortfall to be able to hold on to the rental for an extended time to allow it to appreciate and the rent to rise. In my calculation, I figured that if I put the money in a savings account to earn interest over the years, the financial benefit to me would be minimal. On the other hand, if I used that money to support my newly acquired rental, which I knew would appreciate in value over the years, my money would have been put to better use and I would benefit more. I had information showing that California home prices, on average, doubled every ten years.

I also looked at the Rule of 72, which is loosely used to estimate the years it will take for the value of the home to double. Simply stated, the Rule of 72 says that if you divide 72 by the average rate of home appreciation in the area, you can get an idea of the number of years it will take for the value of the home to double. With Riverside's average appreciation rate of 7% at the time of purchase, I estimated that it would take ten years. With that kind of appreciation, the possibility of getting a good return on my money was higher than if I had saved the money in a bank account.

So, what kind of returns are necessary when choosing an area in which to invest? It is important to assess your financial situation carefully to determine the amount of risk you can take without putting your investment portfolio in financial danger. As a beginner investor, you should invest in properties where you have positive cash flow to get a positive annual rate of return on your investment. The annual rate of return on investment can quickly be arrived at by taking the annual rent you collect and subtracting the expenses you incur to hold the asset. Divide that number by the money paid to buy the rental property. The resulting percentage is your rate of return on investment. A positive number is your goal, and the higher, the better. A big percentage of new investors avoid investing for appreciation and rather go for the cash flow approach. Most areas with positive cash flow have lower appreciation rates, but if you hold on to the rental property for a long time, you come out as a winner.

Other numbers to focus on when choosing an area are net operating income for the property, cash on cash return, debt service coverage ratio, and capitalization rate in the area. These terms are explained in detail below. They are very important when getting into multiple-family investing.

## Rent Control Regulations

There are states and local authorities that impose rent controls on rentals within their jurisdiction. When researching areas, pay attention to tenant laws since they can affect how you collect or raise rent on your property. The laws may also restrict you from evicting non-paying tenants or tenants who don't take good care of the property. Many investors avoid investing in states and cities that have rent control laws. Those laws limit how much you can raise rents in a given period. An investor who buys an apartment building intending to do renovations and raise rents thereafter to recoup the money spent may end up failing to achieve his financial goals if the laws forbid raising rents. An area's restrictive rental regulations negatively affect the income you can collect and may increase expenses greatly, lowering the net operating income. Value addition is one of the most common approaches investors use to grow their portfolios. With properties located in rent control areas, the strategy becomes hard to implement.

## Neighborhood Characteristics And Classification

The adage is that in real estate investing, nothing is more important than the location of the asset; it is location, location, location that matters. After you decide on the metropolitan area, city, or county, start focusing on picking a neighborhood. The neighborhood in which you choose to invest is critical to your success. A good or bad neighborhood is determined by a combination of things that you, as an investor alone, cannot change. Characteristics that define a neighborhood include crime rates, schools, amenities, infrastructure, income levels, and how stringent local regulations govern rental properties. If you choose to buy a rental property in a bad neighborhood, you will have a hard time getting good tenants. You, as an individual investor, can't lower crime rates or improve school performance or the neighborhood's infrastructure.

The importance of investing in a neighborhood with positive characteristics cannot be over-emphasized. You can buy a beaten-down rental property in a bad neighborhood, renovate it, and make it look the best in the neighborhood, but you cannot rehabilitate the bad neighborhood to change its character. The appraised value of the property will be greatly affected by the neighborhood in which it is located. The property will not be as desirable as a similar rental in a good neighborhood. Two similar buildings, one located in a good neighborhood and the other in a bad neighborhood, will have very different assessed values, with the one in a good neighborhood valued higher and rented for higher rent.

Commercial real estate places much weight on neighbor hood types, which are assigned based on the characteristics stated above. Neighborhoods are classified as A, B, C, or D. Areas with an A classification are the most sought after by tenants, and D neighborhoods are the least desirable. A rental unit in a D neighborhood will not get good renters, while one in an A neighborhood will attract renters possessing good qualities. Rents will be lower in a D neighborhood and higher in an A neighborhood. Renters with high incomes will avoid living in D neighborhoods that are usually crime-ridden, with marginal-performing schools and fewer public amenities.

Class A neighborhoods are characterized by having nationally recognized high-end stores such as Trader Joe's and Nordstrom. For investors researching out-of-state areas, these are the characteristics that you could look for to get an idea of the neighborhood classification. If searching using the internet, look to see if there are high-end national stores in the neighborhood. If there are other apartment complexes nearby, look at the amenities offered and the rents charged to get an idea of the building and neighborhood classification. Other information, like the median household incomes and crime rates, can also help determine the neighborhood type. Incomes in Class A areas are higher than in Class B, C, or D neighborhoods. Crime rates are also lower, and schools are ranked higher.

Class B and C neighborhoods are characterized by a large middle-class population with modest consumption habits.

Stores in these areas tend to include national discount chains frequented by middle-income earners. Typical stores include Walmart, Target, Lowes, and Home Depot. Homes in the neighborhood have well-attended yards with tree-lined streets, neighborhood parks, and street infrastructure.

Class D neighborhoods tend to have characteristics that are opposite of what is used to describe Class A neighborhoods. The crime rates are higher; the schools tend to be low performing, they lack good neighborhood stores, and they have few public amenities such as parks and street furniture. The yards are usually unattended with no landscaping and there are no street trees.

## Building Classification

In commercial real estate, which includes apartments, commercial, office buildings, and self-storage facilities, building classification takes on even greater importance. Like neighborhoods, commercial buildings are classified as A, B, C, and D, with each class having distinguishing characteristics.

Class A apartment buildings are nicer, and newer with many modern amenities like an on-site gym, swimming pool, office with printers, fax machines, and meeting rooms for use by tenants to conduct their personal business. These buildings attract high-income earners, and they fetch high rents. Apartment tenants tend to be capable of buying houses based on their earnings but choose to rent for various personal reasons. Tenants usually stay for a short time and move once they have achieved their financial goals. Class A apartment buildings are typically located in class A neighborhoods with high-income households.

Class B apartment buildings are between twenty and forty years old, and they don't have as many amenities as those provided in Class A apartment complexes. The tenants are typically working middle class with good jobs and decent incomes. They are capable of buying houses but may be in the process of saving for the down payment. The household incomes are lower than in Class A areas but typically above the median incomes of the Statistical Metropolitan Area or SMA.

Class C apartment buildings typically are over fifty years old with few amenities and mechanical systems that tend to be aging. Tenants are working-class individuals with incomes lower than the SMA's median. Single-family homes also tend to be older, built over fifty years ago, and priced within a range that lower-income earning workers can afford. Tenants occupying rental units tend to stay in the units for a long time. They are known to weather economic downturns better than tenants in Class A and B buildings because their jobs are usually essential blue-collar jobs that don't get cut during recessions.

Class D buildings are the least desirable for investors because they come with a lot of problems and a higher risk of losing the money invested. They are in rundown D neighborhoods with high rates of crime, and they attract bad characters, like drug dealers. Neighborhood incomes are the lowest in the SMA and are usually below the Federal poverty level. The rents are the lowest in any specific geographic area, and buildings are usually not well maintained. The capitalization rates for these buildings are usually higher than average due to the inherent risks involved and, therefore, are cheap to buy.

When researching an area to invest in, it is important to consider all these classifications. The character of the neighborhood will affect the value and profitability of the asset you buy. The positive thing is that the necessary research can be done remotely, and most of the information can be found online and is free.

# Chapter 24

## Gathering Information: My Experiences with Area Research

Having gone through the process of choosing areas to invest in several times, I can share the lessons I learned. Once you have picked an area to invest in, the focus turns to gathering as much detailed information as you can about the area. An initial thorough investigation of the area does not have to involve travel to the area or extended time away from home. You can use the internet to search and collect most of the information needed to make a meaningful investing decision.

New real estate investors make major mistakes that can be catastrophic. One of those mistakes is failing to research the area carefully and thoroughly before deciding to invest. Avoid making decisions on impulse so as not to incur unnecessary major losses. It is important to eliminate implicit biases about an area in decision-making. Hence, strictly use the facts and don't fall in love or dislike an area when the information suggests otherwise.

It is common for an investor to look at photographs of an apartment building and fall in love with it, investing money even though the building is in a crime-ridden neighborhood or in an area with other negative characteristics. In such cases, the chances of losing money on the investment are greatly increased.

You should get the area's detailed information on demographics, incomes, home appreciation in the neighborhood, schools, crime rates, rents, vacancy rates, and other aspects of the neighborhood. As I have stated above, property prices and rents are affected by how good the neighborhood ranks in those vital areas.

While I was conducting due diligence, I collected information on different areas from the seminars and real estate club meetings I attended, and I spent time carefully studying the information. I read countless reports on areas around the country. I combined the information in the publications with that I gathered from the internet to make decisions. Nowadays, investor club meetings are held on Zoom as webinars or podcasts. There is a lot of information that is given out to attendees that can be used to research an area.

You could also contact the local Chamber of Commerce office, local real estate brokers, and property managers to get the relevant information. Local newspaper websites publish information that is specific to the area, which may include demographic data, incomes, new businesses setting up shops, schools, economic opportunity zones, and so on. Such information is relevant to events that are happening or are about to happen soon. City Council and City Planning Commission decisions about future real estate projects are reported in local newspapers. This information can aid you in making sound investing decisions.

Other sources of information include State, County, and City government offices and websites. Those government agencies have information about planned developments, incomes, demographics, schools, businesses, and transportation systems in their jurisdictions. You can also find geographic information system maps and photos of the area on the websites.

If the jurisdiction has regulations that are specifically applicable to just a few blocks, the map will identify those blocks. Counties and cities develop specific plan regulations that are only applicable to a particular area and may be different from rules applied in other areas of the jurisdiction. Such specific rules may have restrictions on apartments or other real estate that you are interested in buying, and thus, you need to know about them. For those interested in investing in opportunity zones, the locations and the incentives offered can be collected from government offices or government websites. The Federal Government also has plenty of information that is free to access. Various information categories up to street and block level can be found on the Census Bureau website (www.factfinder.census.gov.)

Private company websites collect and publish useful information that is, in most cases, free of charge. Google allows you to view maps and photos of an area miles away from your home while sitting in your living room. Navigating the website, you can take a tour of the neighborhood you want to invest in. Also, on Zillow and Trulia websites, you can get an idea of the real estate market trends in an area. From experience, I have found that although the home values and rents displayed on those websites are estimates, the actual numbers tend to be within ten and fifteen percent of the actual sale or rental values.

Other websites that have useful research information include

www.Rentometer.com

www.apartments.com

www.Rentrange.com

www.loopnet.com

www.crexi.com

www.costar.com

www.realtor.com

www.apartmentlist.com

www.marcusmillichap.com

www.walkscore.com

www.crimemapping.com

www.neighborhoodscout.com

&

www.zumper.com,

## Know The Real Estate Cycles

While studying an area, it is crucial to identify the prevailing real estate cycle or phase. Real estate goes through phases that are characterized by high to low levels of activity and price fluctuations. The four cycles are recession, recovery, expansion, and hyper-supply. The phases tend to mirror strengths in the area's overall economy.

Going through the four cycles/phases strengthens the area's real estate sector. I equate the cycles to a fruit-bearing tree. Once in a while, the tree needs to be shaken to see which fruits are healthy enough to remain attached to the tree. The unhealthy fruits will fall off the tree, thereby retaining only the healthy fruits hanging on the tree. The real estate cycles expose the sectors' weak links.

During the recession cycle, the values are depressed, and properties sit on the market for long periods. The recession cycle is followed by a recovery cycle where values start to rise, and sales activity starts to pick up. During the expansion cycle, activity continues to grow, and newly built properties start to appear on the market. Soon, buyers start to feel like they are missing out on purchases or construction of new units, and the market goes into hyperactivity. The Builders over-build, and buyers compete for homes, resulting in competitive bidding and overpaying for the units. Eventually, the market cools, and the inventory of homes on the market builds up, and prices start to fall. The market then cycles back into the recessionary phase.

The Federal Reserve Board's actions can influence real estate cycles. This was evidenced in the recent past by its actions during the Covid pandemic period and during the 2007-2008 housing crash. In both instances, the Federal Reserve manipulated the interest rates to affect the demand for housing. Interest rates were lowered, which triggered a demand for housing, and as the demand for housing went up, so did the prices. During the housing crash, the Federal Reserve used interest rate cuts to stimulate housing demand, which had sunk to dangerous lows. Conversely, if the housing market is in an expansion cycle, the Federal Reserve's actions can reverse the market into a recessionary cycle by raising interest rates. The Federal Reserve's mandate to ensure maximum employment and stable prices was established through the Federal Reserve Act.

Knowing what cycle the market is in is important because it can save you money in the short and long run. If you buy property when the area is expanding, you will be competing with many buyers and are likely to overpay. On the other hand, if you buy during the recessionary phase, you can get the property for less money and will be competing with fewer people. Sellers are more willing to negotiate price reductions in a recessionary phase.

## Screening Tenants

I have found that screening tenants is as important as researching areas to invest in. You should not cut corners when screening your future tenants. The right tenant for your property can be the key determinant as to whether you succeed as an investor or not. I have my property managers thoroughly screen the prospective tenants. I asked them to give me details of the tenants' employment earnings and history, credit history, and their past rental history. I use that information to decide as to which tenant I approve to rent my houses. By looking at that information, you can spot red flags that signal future problem tenants.

Thoroughly check the references to determine the character of the tenant you are going to place in your rental property. Call the employer to make sure that the information on the rental application matches up with what the employer tells you. Tenants with a history of paying their rent late should be avoided, as are tenants who previously left properties in a total mess, requiring a lot of repairs.

Some tenants may have a troubled financial past, such as bankruptcy. Look at their situation in totality and determine the circumstances that caused the bankruptcy. I have rented to tenants with a past bankruptcy, and they turned out to be the best tenants. They paid rent on time, stayed in the property for over five years, and took great care of the rental. They used that time as renters to rebuild their financial history, build a strong credit history, and buy a house when they vacated my property. Such tenants are better at managing risks and are more versed in handling finances due to the past lessons they learned.

I have seen landlords who got tenants off websites like Craigslist or took tenants who were referred to them by word of mouth from acquaintances or church groups and rented to them without checking their history. Those landlords ended up with big expenses on repairs and months of unpaid rent.

A good tenant is not one who is willing to pay the highest rent for your property. Rather, look for a tenant who will pay rent on time and is likely to stay for a long time to save you on the costs related to tenant turnover and repairs. Families with young children attending neighborhood schools are good to rent to. They tend to move less frequently to avoid interrupting schooling for the children. If they must move, they will do so after the school year has ended.

# Chapter 25

## Building a Team

Real estate investing is a team sport that involves different players having different skill sets. One of the initial steps to take once you decide to get into real estate investing is to build a team. The team you put together will save you time and money. You will not be searching for people to handle problems every time you encounter one. If, while starting out, you belong to a real estate investment club, ask club members for referral names of contractors, realtors, mortgage brokers, property managers, and other professionals. You have the advantage of choosing from a pool of tried and tested professionals who can reduce your risks tremendously.

During the process of acquiring properties, I established a list of individuals that I could call upon before and after I took possession of the property. The real estate investment network that I was a member of had realtors, property managers, insurance agents, inspectors, and contractors that I could pick from to form my team in the areas I invested in. These were professionals who had been screened prior by the investment club and had good reviews from investors. Those investors were always willing to recommend good people to join my team. Your team should include:

## Real Estate Broker

Brokers have for-sale property listings, and they have access to the multiple listing service. If you are looking to invest in a faraway area, a broker can bring you properties to buy that meet your criteria. Brokers may also know properties that are for sale but not advertised on the multiple listing services, which are commonly known as pocket listings. Having a good relationship with brokers in the area you want to invest in allows you to get advanced knowledge of properties that are up for sale even before they get on the market. With such properties, you will have less competition, and you are likely to buy the property at a favorable price.

## Property Manager

A property manager brings to the team professional knowledge of how to rent the property and handle tenant matters and repairs. They know the regulations applicable in the area. Having a property manager frees up your time to work on other things that will likely make you more money than what you would save managing the property yourself.

Property management should be left to someone with the knowledge and experience of managing similar properties in the local area. A property with 150 units requires a property manager who is experienced in handling apartment complexes of a similar size. A property manager who specializes in smaller buildings of 20 units will not be able to manage a larger complex of hundreds of units. The manager should have a thorough knowledge of the local rental conditions, including the going rents being charged, the vacancy rates, and the concessions being offered. To succeed, you must research and thoroughly know your competition, and for that, you rely on your property manager.

### Attorney

Attorneys understand both the local real estate laws and laws governing syndications and joint ventures. If you are to include investors in your purchase, the attorney will help navigate through Securities and Exchange Commission regulations. They will also prepare legal documents such as the Private Placement Memorandum and agreements spelling out how ownership of the property will be divided. An attorney will review your contracts and advise you when negotiating loan terms.

### Accountant

The Internal Revenue Service regulations for commercial investing are many and complex. They are better assigned to an individual who knows those rules in and out, greatly reducing the chances of being audited. An accountant or other tax professional can also do a cost segregation analysis of the property, which can result in tax savings. Cost segregation is allowed under IRS rules for apartment investors to accelerate their depreciation and thereby improve their cash flow.

### Inspector

Inspectors are crucial for both single-family residential and multifamily purchases. With a trained eye, an inspector can identify issues that you, as an untrained purchaser, cannot see.

Avoid completing a purchase before the property has been inspected. The inspection could be completed during the initial due diligence period or could be required later by including it as a contingency clause in the purchase agreement.

The inspector should check for any additions or alterations that were not permitted by the local authority or homeowner association. Local Building and Planning Departments have permit records for new construction as well as additions and alterations. It is very common to ignore such unpermitted work and assume that everything in the home complies with local regulations and homeowners association (HOA) by-laws. Work that involves added or reduced building square footage, changes or additions to the electrical, plumbing, or mechanical systems, and patio covers, swimming pools, and structures detached from the main house require building permits.

Home buyers who fail to identify or ignore such additions and alterations do inherit all the risks that come with unpermitted construction. The homeowner may be held liable for accidents resulting from the unpermitted work; insurance companies may refuse to insure the home. Also, improvements to the property must be reported to the county assessor. Hence, unreported additions could result in a big tax bill and fines if discovered later.

If unpermitted work is found, the buyer can ask the seller to secure the building permits prior to closing or negotiate a price reduction in the amount necessary to legalize the unpermitted work.

## Contractor Or Handyman

Like having an inspector, it is necessary to have a contractor on your team. This is the person who will do any construction or repair work required on the property. A contractor can also estimate the cost of repairs and come up with the cost for capital expenditures. You should do your due diligence with your contractor and inspector to know what repairs will be needed and the cost of those repairs. When negotiating a price with the seller, you can bring up the cost of the repairs to lower the asking price.

## Appraiser And/Or Underwriter

The value of single-family residences and rental properties with four or fewer units is determined by conducting an appraisal. Most single-family residential loans will not be funded unless the value of the property exceeds the loan amount. If the value is less than the loan amount, the buyer can pay the difference between the two to complete the sale.

For apartment properties, the value is determined by considering the net operating income and capitalization rate. The net operating income is divided by the capitalization rate, and the resulting number is the value of the apartment complex. The team should have someone who knows well how to underwrite commercial properties.

The underwriting process takes all expenses and income generated by the property to come up with the net operating income. To further confirm that you, as a buyer, are not overpaying for the property, you could compare the prices for similar apartment buildings recently sold in the area.

## Lender, Mortgage Broker, Or Banker

Borrowing money is the foundation on which real estate investing stands. We, as investors, build wealth by leveraging money that is not ours by taking ownership of property and paying back the loan over time. It is necessary to have someone on the team to handle purchase loans. A banker or mortgage broker will have up-to-date information on what is happening in the financial world and what types of loans are available at any given time. They will tell you what is needed to qualify for a loan and whether you or the property qualifies for the loan. This is true whether you are buying a single-family residence or an apartment complex.

Having someone on the team to handle issues related to financing saves plenty of time in the process. Mortgage brokers know lending requirements from several lenders and can shop around to find the best loan for the property. Regional banks finance a large percentage of commercial properties, and they are a good party to have on the team. Loan brokers specializing in residential lending rarely handle loans for apartments.

Once the team is in place, it becomes a matter of picking up a phone and calling any of them to handle or get advice on any aspect of investing without spending much time searching for the right individual. With a knowledgeable team of individuals, you can avoid one of the common mistakes investors make, which is to seek advice from relatives or friends who may not know much about real estate and, in many cases, would only discourage you from pursuing your goals. In real estate investing, your success is closely tied to the team you put together.

# Chapter 26

# Loans

## Loan Application Process And Credit

I have stated earlier that loans are the backbone of building wealth in real estate investing. Mortgages have been around for many years, and they are credited for lifting many people in America from poverty into the middle class and even into the super-rich class. Racial minority groups that were prohibited from purchasing real estate did not benefit from those mortgages at the time. The vast gap in wealth today between racial minorities and whites can be partly attributed to the thirty-year mortgage that enabled people to buy real estate, many using a thirty-year mortgage to build generational wealth.

## 30-Year Fixed Rate Mortgage

More than anything else, the 30-year fixed-rate mortgage is credited for lifting many American families from poverty and into the middle and upper class. This mortgage type was introduced during the Great Depression in the 1930s. Prior to its introduction, mortgages had a shorter pay-off period of three or five years. Additionally, the mortgages did not amortize, which meant that at the end of the period, the borrower had to come up with a huge amount of money to pay off the loan. This created a big problem during the Great Depression since not many people could raise the money to pay off their mortgages. As a result, foreclosures were rampant. Many people lost their homes and the money they invested in the homes.

To address this problem and stabilize the real estate sector and the national economy as a whole, the federal government created the Home Owners' Loan Corporation. This corporation later evolved into the present-day Fannie Mae and Freddie Mac, both of which have since been powerful players in the US mortgage industry. Without their backing, the 30-year mortgage would not exist as we know it today.

There are many advantages the 30-year fixed rate mortgage brings to home ownership, and they include:

- Spreading out the payments over 30 years, which in turn results in lower monthly payments. Shorter pay-off periods, such as 5-year or 3-year pay-off periods, result in higher monthly payments, which keep individuals from owning homes.
- Establishing monthly payment predictability. The homeowner can budget for housing expenses without worrying about spikes in payments.
- The fixed-rate mortgages have prevented a complete collapse of the real estate sector during financial downturns. During the 2007-2008 Great Recession, homeowners who had adjustable mortgages couldn't afford the payments that adjusted higher as interest rates rose. As such, many homes were lost to foreclosure, which sent a shock wave throughout the economy, even though the percentage of adjustable mortgages during that time is estimated to be between 20% and 25% of all mortgages issued by lenders.

- Generational wealth creation for American families. With access to loans and gradually paying the loan over a 30-year period, many families acquired homes that have remained in their families and passed down as heirlooms or established a foundation or capital for buying other real estate.
- The mortgages can be refinanced to lower the monthly payments if the interest rates fall.

The 30-year mortgage has been blamed for creating a shortage of resale homes and, therefore, resulting in a housing crisis because people are not forced to sell their homes more often. It is argued that shorter payoff periods of 5-year or 3-years, for instance, would result in many more homes being available for buyers and lower home prices. I consider this argument to be outweighed by the advantages realized through having longer payoff periods.

Additionally, the supply of homes on the market can be increased through the relaxation of local regulations, especially zoning laws. Those laws can be changed to allow more housing units in a given area, say, an acre. Zoning laws restrict how many homes can be built on an acre, using allowable minimum lot sizes and building setbacks.

I have touched upon the importance of having a lender or loan broker on the team. The loan types and qualification requirements are varied, and having someone knowledgeable on the team makes the process much easier. Start by talking to your lender or loan broker about your goals and the type of property you wish to buy. By explaining to them what you are looking for, they can find loans that suit your goals. When buying single-family residences, it is advisable to get pre-qualified before starting to look for properties. With commercial properties, searching for a lender by your loan broker can start after you locate a property.

## Single-Family Residential Loans

The loan application process is one of the steps that is necessary to complete before you buy a house. For lending purposes, rental properties with up to four units are categorized as single-family residences. Lenders have different loan qualification requirements for primary residences and rental houses. The requirements are more stringent for rental houses, and interest rates are higher than for primary residences.

Loans for duplexes, triplexes, fourplexes, townhouses, and condominiums are considered single-family loans and tend to have similar loan requirements and terms. Loan terms are different for financing properties with five or more units.

So, what is the difference between a duplex, triplex, fourplex, townhouse and a condominium? A duplex is characterized by two homes on a single lot having separate entrances, kitchens, and living areas. The homes may be attached or detached. The tax collector assigns a single parcel identification number to the lot even though the homes may have separate mailing addresses. Generally, the property is under one owner, although lately, some states are considering allowing more than single ownership to remedy a severe housing shortage.

A triplex has three units situated on a single lot. Similar to a duplex, it has separate entrances, living arrangements, and kitchens. The assessor assigns one parcel identification number, but the units may have separate addresses.

A fourplex, or a quad, has four residential units with separate entrances, kitchens, and living arrangements. All units are on a single lot with the same parcel identification number.

A condominium building has several residential units constructed on the same lot, with separate entrances, kitchens, and living arrangements. The property is typically assigned one address. Each unit has an identifying letter, such as unit A, unit B, and so on. Each owner pays the unit's assessed property taxes. The units have shared interior walls and a common roof. All condominium owners share the outdoor areas. Condominium owners form an owner association, which takes care of the common areas and other shared amenities. The land beneath the building is jointly owned by all unit owners through the HOA.

Townhouses are characterized by separate entrances, separate kitchens, and separate living arrangements. The houses have shared interior walls that separate the units. Although the buildings may appear to be constructed on a single lot, townhouses have separate assessor parcel numbers. It is common to find townhouses in densely populated areas where they are constructed with multiple levels with several units attached to each other in a row formation. Some townhome developments have an owner association that takes care of the common areas and amenities. The units are individually owned, including the land on which each townhouse is constructed.

## Credit Scores

When you apply for a loan, the lender will evaluate your application to assess the risks that the lender will take by lending you money. Will you be able to pay back the loan, or will you default on the loan and cause a loss to the lender? As a borrower, you use leverage to acquire property to build wealth, and the lender charges interest and fees to make a profit. It is a win-win situation.

There are two widely used scores in the lending industry: the Fair Isaac Corporation score (FICO) and the VantageScore, which was developed through a corporation between Experian, TransUnion, and Equifax credit reporting agencies. Both scores track the borrower's payment history, amount of credit, and the length of the credit history to calculate the score. The minimum score that those agencies can report is 300, and the maximum score is 850. Lenders set a minimum credit score necessary to approve a borrower for a loan.

Fair Isaac Corporation gathers information on your debts, including credit cards, personal loans, and car loans. The score is calculated using the number and mix of credit accounts you have. Also included in the mix is how you are using the credit on those accounts and how long you have had the accounts. The agencies look at how much of the credit you are granted is being used and if you are paying back the money as agreed. Each of those items is assigned a different weight in calculating the score with the payment history weighing more than any other item.

FICO and VantageScore assign different weights to those items. Fair Isaac Corporation score assigns 35% of your credit score to your payment history, 30% to the amount of debt you have, 15% to the length of your credit history, 10% to the amount of new credit, and 10% to the type and mix of the credit you have.

On the other hand, VantageScore Model 4.0 uses the following numbers: 41% payment history, 20% age or length of credit, 20% credit utilization, 6% balances, 11% recently opened credit, and 2% available credit.

Both FICO and VantageScore can be increased or decreased by changing any of those variables that go into the calculation. For instance, you could lower the balances you owe on any of the accounts to raise your score. Having that in mind, it is advisable not to open new credit accounts or use more credit on the accounts once you submit a loan application.

Once you fill out a loan application, the lender will get a copy of your credit report from one or more of the credit reporting agencies. The three widely used credit reporting agencies are TransUnion, Experian, and Equifax. Each of those agencies calculates the credit score differently, and therefore, even though they are looking at the same information, the score they report will be different. Some lenders choose to get reports from all three and then use the middle score, discarding the lowest and highest scores. Others add the three scores and use the average. All three agencies also report the VantageScore in addition to the FICO score.

Lenders get the credit report any time after you sign a form authorizing them to access information in your credit report. To avoid wasting time working on a loan application with no chance of being approved, lenders pull the credit report at the start of the application process.

Be prepared to provide additional documents once the credit report is pulled to collaborate information in your credit report. The lender will also ask for documents verifying your income and monthly statements from your creditors. For most people, income verification documents include W2s, Federal Income taxes filed in the prior two years, 1099 forms showing self-employment income, bank statements, and copies of recent checks for your self-employment work. The lender reviews these documents, and if questions come up during the review, the lender will want you to clarify. Clarification can be in the form of a letter, a phone call explanation, e-mails, or mailing the required clarification documents.

Lenders use all the information they collect to calculate the debt-to-income ratio. This ratio determines whether you have enough money to pay back your debts based on your income. Each lender sets the debt-to-income ratio they accept. The acceptable ratio also depends on whether the loan will have to comply with standards set by the Federal agencies that buy the loans from lenders such as FANNIE MAE and FREDDIE MAC.

Occasionally, lenders will change the debt ratios necessary to qualify for a loan based on the type of job you do, how long you have been at the job, and prospects of advancing to a higher-paying position or getting a raise. The lenders may, therefore, approve a loan with a higher debt ratio if they are convinced that you will be able to earn more in the future based on your situation.

If the debt ratio turns out to be higher than the lender accepts, you could lower it by providing additional income for consideration. This can be done by taking on a second job in your free time away from the regular job. It would require planning ahead since the length of time spent working at the job is considered before such income can be used in the calculation. Most lenders want to see at least two years with the employer. The alternative approach would be to bring on a co-buyer whose income can be used in the calculation.

In addition to the income, the lender will have to verify your assets. The more valuable assets you own, the lower the risk number assigned to you by the lender. Submitting your bank and brokerage statements, titles for properties you own, and other valuables is a way to support your application. As you can imagine, the loan application process can be stressful. Beforehand preparation by gathering the necessary documents and having knowledge of the information you will be asked to provide greatly lowers the stress level.

## Types Of Single-Family Loans

It was in graduate school at the University of Washington that I was first introduced to how real estate is financed in the United States of America. It was in the Real Estate Finance and Development class that I took, which met twice weekly very early in the morning. The class was the first crack into a window that let me investigate how the USA has been able to have many of its people own real estate and how that has moved many people from lower income to middle income.

There are several loan types available to investors and the type of loan you end up getting will be dependent on the type of asset you are seeking to finance or acquire. Some of the loans are government-backed and are referred to as government-sponsored enterprise (GSE) loans. GSEs are semi-private government agencies created to ensure that there is money available in the markets to finance home purchases. They accomplish this by buying mortgages from banks and other mortgage lenders and packaging the loans into securities that are sold to investors, usually on the stock exchanges. The sale of the packaged securities generates money to make loans to new borrowers. The GSEs themselves don't directly lend money to borrowers. Those semi-government agencies are under the overall supervision of the Federal Housing Finance Agency (FHFA).

Three government agencies participate in this exercise of ensuring that credit is available for home purchases. First is the Federal Home Loan Mortgage Corporation (Freddie Mac). Second is the Federal National Mortgage Association (Fannie Mae), and the third is the Government National Mortgage Association (Ginnie Mae). Below are the most frequently used loans for residential purchase:

1. The Federal Housing Administration (FHA) loan program was established to enable middle- and low-income home buyers to purchase homes. The loans require a low down-payment of at least 3.5% of the purchase price and a credit

score in the mid-six hundred. The FHA insures the lender against losses in case of borrower default. If the borrower defaults on the loan and the property is repossessed, the FHA pays the lender any deficit amount of the outstanding loan and the proceeds from the sale of the repossessed property. Because of the low downpayment, the borrower must pay mortgage insurance. The money from those insurance premiums is used to pay the amounts FHA pays lenders in case of loan default.

2. Department of Veterans Affairs (VA) loans. These loans are offered to active-duty military personnel, military veterans, and surviving military spouses. They require no downpayment, and unlike FHA loans, the borrower does not have to pay mortgage insurance.
3. United States Department of Agriculture (USDA) loans. These loans are offered in rural America and are intended to make homeownership affordable. Borrowers pay a lower downpayment and are not required to carry mortgage insurance.
4. Conventional loans: These loans are different from the three loan types described above in that they are not backed by the GSEs. The lender does not have to abide by the requirements of the government and lenders establish their own qualification requirements. The downpayment required varies from lender to lender, as do interest rates

and loan terms. Lenders may abide by the GSE requirements of their choosing, especially if they want to sell the loans to those government agencies. Conventional loans that meet the Fannie Mae and Freddie Mac requirements are referred to as conforming loans.

## Residential Construction Loans

If you are to develop property instead of buying an existing, already-built house, you will be applying for a construction loan. Construction loans are different from the traditional residential loans for already-built homes. These are the most common loans offered to finance house construction:

1. Construction-to-permanent loan. This kind of loan is used to build the house, and once construction is complete, the loan converts into a traditional long-term home loan. No new loan application is required. The loan can be used to buy land on which the home will be constructed. The loans typically have an eighteen-month duration. Because they carry a higher risk of default, the interest rates tend to be higher. The lender follows the construction progress, and disbursements are made after completion of previously determined stages of construction.
2. Construction-only loan. This loan is granted to build the house, and all the borrowed money must be paid back once complete. That means that the owner has to go through a

loan application process all over again to finance the property long-term, usually for thirty years.

3. End-loan: This type of loan is granted after the borrower closes out the construction loan. The loans are similar to those owners get to buy existing homes, and payments are stretched out for fifteen or thirty years.
4. Owner-builder loans: These loans are offered to owners who act as their owner-contractors building their homes. The owner-contractor has to meet certain requirements, including being a licensed contractor with the required education and experience.
5. Rehabilitation or bridge loans cover the construction costs of rehabilitating an existing building. They are commonly used by house flippers and tend to be for a short duration, usually no more than two years.
6. The Federal Housing Administration created FHA 203(k) loans that combine the cost of buying a home and the rehabilitation costs. This loan type is a favorite of investors who don't want to get a purchase loan and a second loan to cover rehabilitation costs. The FHA allows borrowers to borrow up to 110% of the after-rehab value of the property.

## Multi-Family Residential Loans

There is a difference between loans for single-family residences and those for multi-family residences. I stated that single-family residences, for loan application purposes, include residences that are less than four units, generally called fourplexes or quadplexes. A loan for five or more units is considered an application for a multi-family or a commercial loan. For single-family residences, the applicant is evaluated for approval of the loan, and their personal finances are central to the loan approval. For commercial loan applications, the income and expenses from the building play a crucial role in approving the loan.

There are many types of commercial loans, and in this discussion, I will discuss the most commonly used loan types. I will focus on non-recourse loans, and I will assume that the loan amount will be at least $1 million, which is the minimum amount required for the loan to qualify as non-recourse. After all, most reasonable-sized apartment complexes sell for over one million dollars.

For clarity, a non-recourse loan is secured by a specific asset, and that asset serves as collateral. The lender can't go after the borrower's other assets to recover money borrowed if there is a deficiency. With a recourse loan, on the other hand, the borrower guarantees the loan, and if there is a deficiency, the lender can move to recover the loss by going after the borrower's other assets.

Most apartment buyers would not be qualified for a loan over one million dollars using only their personal earned income. Some of the commercial loans originated by lenders are sold to the Federal National Mortgage Association or Fannie Mae, while others are kept by loan originators, usually a local or regional bank, and are referred to as portfolio loans.

With most of the multi-family residential loans, the primary focus is on the property or asset itself. The asset's finances are evaluated to see if it makes financial sense to make the loan. The income generated by the property must be enough to pay all the expenses involved, including servicing the mortgage and having some money left over for a reserve fund.

Proving that the property is financially viable requires getting financial information from the property owner, broker, or management company. Income and expenses are documented on a trailing 12, trailing 9, 6, or trailing 3. The documents are also referred to as T-12, T-9, T-6, T-3, or Profit and Loss (P&L) statements. These documents show the total income from all the rents collected from each rental unit, plus any other miscellaneous income collected that is not rent, such as payment for parking spaces, late fees, and laundry facilities.

Also included on the documents is income from the ratio utility billing system or R.U.B.S. The ratio utility billing system, by estimate, allocates utility costs according to how much each apartment unit uses through an established formula. The formula considers the number of people in the unit, the size of the unit, the number of bedrooms and bathrooms, and appliances such as washers and dryers. A tenant who uses more water, gas, or electricity pays more than one who uses less. Some landlords use the traditional method, where each tenant pays a flat fee for the utilities.

The profit and loss (or T-12, T-9, T-6, or T-3) statement contains information on gross scheduled income, which assumes that all units are rented without vacancies. Miscellaneous incomes are added and vacancies are subtracted to come up with the effective gross income.

Once the effective gross income is calculated, the lender will want to see the expenses incurred to run the apartments. The expenses vary for each building or apartment complex, but they usually include such things as property taxes, utilities, contracts, management fees, legal fees, maintenance costs, salaries, and administrative costs.

The next important number the lender will want to see is the net operating income (NOI). This is calculated by taking the total effective gross income collected and subtracting the expenses. This number is important because it is used to determine the value of the property for which the loan is being sought. The NOI is divided by the capitalization rate to determine the value of the property. For an apartment complex having a net operating income of $100,000 and a capitalization rate of 5 percent, its value is $2 million. The lender will not make the loan if the determined value is less than the loan applied for.

Also, by using the NOI, the debt service coverage ratio (DSCR) is calculated. From the net operating income, the loan to finance the asset purchase is paid back. The lenders want to see a DSCR of not less than 1.25. For instance, if the apartment building has a net operating income of $12,500 every year, the amount going toward debt payment for the year should not exceed $10,000 to maintain a 1.25 DSCR. That is determined by having $12,500 divided by $10,000, which gives you a 1.25 debt service coverage ratio.

Briefly, the lenders will look at the following matrix while evaluating the application to decide on whether to approve the loan:

1. Value of the property: This is calculated by taking the asset's net operating income divided by the capitalization rate, or cap rate. The capitalization rate is expressed as a percentage. It shows the expected return on investment and estimates the rate at which the net operating income pays back the asset purchase price every year.

2. Net Operating Income (NOI): The lender will want to see the NOI as explained above. The higher the NOI, the greater the possibility that the loan will be approved.
3. Loan-to-value (LTV): This is crucial in approving loans for both apartments and single-family residences. It is derived by dividing the mortgage amount borrowed by the property value. Lenders usually want to see an LTV value above 75 percent. If the appraised value of the property is the same as the loan amount, the lender may ask for a down

payment of 25 percent to reach the desired 75 percent LTV.

4. Debt Service Coverage Ratio (DSCR): As stated earlier, the desired debt service coverage ratio by lenders is 1.25 or greater. That ratio signifies that after paying your mortgage from the NOI, you will have a surplus equivalent to 25% of the debt service amount, which can be used for reserves or other purposes. With a DSCR of 1.25, for every dollar of debt service, the property generates $1.25 in NOI. Or $1.00 goes to debt service and $0.25 remains as surplus. If the DSCR number is 1, then the income from the property only pays the expenses and mortgage with no money left over. A ratio of less than 1 indicates that the apartment complex is running on a deficit.
5. Cash-on-cash (COC) return: The lenders prefer to see a positive number, usually in double digits. This cash-on-cash number is important to the borrower, especially if the asset is bought through syndication by several investors pooling money together. The investors are paid distributions monthly or quarterly if there is a positive COC return number. Cash on cash return is calculated by dividing cash flow, or cash left after paying debts, by the cash you invested in the asset. If you bought apartment units for $100,000 and you put down $25,000, if your cash flow after paying your debt is $5,000, your cash-on-cash return is 20

percent. As a syndicator, you want to see a cash-on-cash return number above 12 percent.

Numbers and calculations play a vital role in securing a loan for apartments. Once you find a multi-family building you are interested in, you will have to do those calculations. The process is called underwriting the deal. Earlier, I talked about having someone on the team who could underwrite deals to make sure that they meet lenders' requirements. The underwriting process also shows which apartment deals make financial sense and are suitable to invest in. It is common for the underwriter to evaluate dozens of properties before a good deal is found. Fortunately, there is software on the market that can help quickly underwrite deals.

The primary focus is on the property's financials, but of secondary importance is the loan principal applicant's experience in real estate and their net worth. Lenders want to see that the individual applying for the loan has some experience investing in real estate. For new investors in commercial real estate, this will mean that an experienced investor will have to be brought in to be the applicant. The experienced investor will take a percentage of ownership of the property in return.

The principal applicant should have substantial assets equal to or more than the loan amount being sought. For beginner investors, this is another reason why they have to bring in a sponsor to stand in as the applicant. Experienced investors can make money by standing in as applicants for assets that show promise of being successful and profitable.

My personal observation is that loans are a principal component of real estate investing. During my education, loans were always front and center in the discussion of acquiring investment properties. Acquiring an investment property using a bad loan will, in most cases, result in losing money on the investment.

There are many loan types for asset purchase that can be structured to fit varying investor financing needs. A loan intended for rehabbing a flip property is structured differently from a loan for a buy-and-hold property. As an investor, you need to decide which loan type is best suited for the property you are buying.

Similarly, if you are buying a house to be rented out for a period not exceeding five years, you need to choose a loan that has a lower monthly payment for the first five years, even though the payment may go up after five years. A property intended for long-term holding, for instance, thirty years, should be financed with loans that are fully amortized with no large increases in monthly payments or balloon payments.

It is important to know the numbers when it comes to getting into a loan. An optimal loan is one that allows you to use the rent collected to pay principal and interest, property taxes, insurance, minor repairs, and money left over to add to reserves. With such a loan, every month, the loan balance will decrease, thereby increasing your net worth. You could spend the entire year vacationing and still end the year wealthier than when you started it.

Adjustable-rate mortgages can be attractive because they tend to start with a lower payment, thereby leaving a bigger chunk of money in your bank account. However, if not structured to suit your investment goals, they can be a dangerous trap and could result in losing your investment. The payment can increase, and the rent collected may not cover the mortgage payment, property taxes, insurance and repair expenses, or other emergencies. You end up not building up your reserves that are needed to cover vacancies and instead, the reserves get depleted. It becomes a matter of time before you can't hold on to the property without borrowing money from other sources. An adjustable mortgage should be structured to limit the payment increases by such actions as putting a cap on how much the interest rate can rise.

# Chapter 27

# Operating Your Investment Asset

## Cash Reserves

Every now and then, you will run into a situation where there is no rental income coming in, or something in the rental unit needs a costly repair. Other incidental expenditures, like legal fees, also come up. The ideal situation is where the rent collected every month covers the expenses after the mortgage is paid. Such a situation is never guaranteed, therefore, to avoid a cash shortage that could result in losing your property, there must be reserve funds that you can access.

Failing to budget for cash reserves is one of the most common mistakes real estate investors make. Whether it is a single-family residence or an apartment, there should be money set aside to cover at least six months of mortgage payments and expenses. Lenders want to see the presence of those funds during the loan processing process. The amount required varies from lender to lender. When underwriting apartment deals, the reserve money must be included in the calculations presented to the lender. The lender will hold those funds in the bank and will require that you replenish the funds as they get spent.

Other than lender-required funds for apartments, money that counts toward reserves could be in different accounts and actively invested. When applying for my mortgages, lenders accepted as reserves, money in my retirement account. I had to prove that I could withdraw the money from my retirement account in case an emergency arose. My employer allowed me to put money in a retirement account and I could take it out as a loan to myself if I had an emergency. In addition, I had money invested in stocks and exchange-traded funds, which the lenders took as reserves.

I always took a more conservative approach to my reserve calculations. I used a formula that set aside at least six months of mortgage payments per property plus three thousand dollars for the make-ready expenses. I estimated that it took forty-five days to find a tenant from the time the unit fell vacant.

There is no one formula to calculate the amount of money needed in the reserve fund. Every rental property owner has different circumstances that determine how much should be set aside. The amount of equivalent funds set aside will depend on factors like the rental market conditions in the area, years since the rental was built or renovated, and the age of the appliances. Each of those factors affects how much money will be spent from the reserve fund.

During the COVID-19 pandemic, the demand for rental units in major rental markets was high, and units stayed on the market for short periods. Due to high rental demand, the amount of money needed to cover vacancies was little. During periods of economic slowdown, more money would be needed in the reserves to cover vacancies. If the rental property is in an area of weak economic activity, the units tend to remain unrented for a long time. In such situations, you need to have a bigger reserve fund.

Also important is the overall condition of the building and the appliances within. If the house is renovated with new appliances, a new roof, or new flooring installed, the money set aside would not have to be high. Appliances have a period when they work perfectly with no need for repairs. A new roof will not require repair work for at least ten years if properly installed. In such instances, the amount of money set aside in the reserve fund can be adjusted lower. On the other hand, if an older home is purchased and no repairs are done after the acquisition, more money should be kept as reserves.

What is true with a renovated house is true with a newly constructed residence. With a new house, you get new appliances that will work for many years without breakage. The roof, plumbing, electrical, and other systems in the house will also function normally for many years. That gives the investor some leeway when it comes to setting aside reserves. The investor may be able to get away with having only three months of reserves. The money would be sufficient to cover vacancies and make-ready repairs after the tenants move out.

## Manage Your Relations With Relatives And Friends

As human beings, we tend to have a soft spot for friends and relatives when they need help, even when such an action will negatively affect our investments. As a landlord, there may come a time when a relative or friend approaches you wanting to occupy your rental unit. This can be an individual decision you make whether to rent to them or not. The advantage of renting to your friend or relative is that you know them very well. You know their character and ways of life. This is not the case when you rent to an unknown tenant. You take a chance that they will turn out to be good tenants.

So, if you feel comfortable that your relative or friend is a good person and will not take advantage of you, then go ahead and rent to them. As a word of caution, you should treat them as you would treat any other tenant. They should sign a lease agreement and enforce the terms of the agreement the same way you would enforce them with any other tenant. Don't allow the rent to be paid late or the property to fall out of maintenance. Real estate investor Engelo Romero said, "Keep your friends close, enemies closer, and family as far away as possible."

Some landlords are unwavering when it comes to renting to friends and relatives. They consider the rental unit to be a business, and they are in it to make a profit. Renting to friends and relatives comes with higher risks and could result in a loss of money. Everything can be going well until the rent is not paid or the property is not taken care of properly. Those are situations where you would have to evict the tenants from your rental, but because of the close personal ties, it becomes difficult to remove a relative or friend. Relatives and friends may also be less inclined to pay rent on time, feeling like they can get away with it. Raising rent to be at market rate also becomes difficult.

Another disadvantage of renting to a relative is the possibility of losing the tax deductions that come with being a landlord. Being able to deduct your rental expenses and depreciation is one of the benefits of owning rental properties. It is important to read IRS Publication 527, which describes in detail all the rules that affect rental properties. If rented to a relative, expenses and depreciation may not be tax deductible. Have a discussion with your tax professional prior to renting to a relative.

## Take Care Of Your Property

Throughout my time as a landlord, I have come to learn that taking good care of the property pays off. A well-maintained property attracts good tenants, whereas neglected rentals attract problem tenants. It is necessary to take care of all the required repairs so that the property does not get into a condition that will discourage potential good tenants with good credit and income.

In addition, if the property is well maintained, the tenant is likely to take care of it well, while unattended properties get neglected by the tenants, reasoning that they found it in bad form anyway. When preparing the rental lease agreement, you should state clearly who is responsible for paying for the cost of repairs and maintenance. It is common for the tenant to maintain the lawn and flower beds.

I have discussed the importance of knowing the landlord-tenant laws in the location you are investing in. You should be aware of the laws that set legally binding requirements between the landlord and the tenant. These laws vary from state to state and even localities. Therefore, know your legal responsibilities, especially when it comes to repairs and evictions. Neglecting certain important repairs could lead to lawsuits that could be costly as is wrongly evicting a tenant.

Between renters during the make-ready period, check everything to make sure they are in proper working condition. Plumbing, mechanical, and electrical systems should be inspected and given a tune-up. It is more time-efficient and a lot cheaper to do the maintenance when the house is vacant. You don't have to schedule maintenance appointments that meet the tenant's, the repair person and your schedule. When the house is vacant, it is easier to schedule several contractors and get more than one or two estimates. It becomes more challenging when you must schedule repair appointments that meet the tenants' time availability.

I have always made sure that I repaired any damage to the walls and, if needed, painted the house with a fresh paint coat. I check and service all major systems like the air conditioning system, the furnace, the plumbing system, the electrical system, smoke, and carbon monoxide detectors. If needed I get the systems tuned up before the tenants move in. For any items that are reaching the end of their life expectancy, I replace them during the vacancy period. I always refurbish the lawn, flower beds, and irrigation system. If the tenant will be responsible for the yard maintenance, I hand over the responsibility when the yard is in perfect form. They will take better care of the yard if it is in top form and well-maintained at the beginning of the lease period.

Once the house is rented, I ask for regular property inspections by the property manager. I get the inspections scheduled every six months and get photographs to document the condition of the rental. For rentals within driving distance, I do regular drive-by inspections to see if from the exterior, the rental is well taken care of. By doing so, I can spot preventive repairs that can be taken care of promptly to avoid costlier repair costs in the future. A small water leak not repaired promptly could spread over a larger area and require removing and replacing larger damaged areas.

## Pay Attention To Local Ordinances

Several times earlier, I talked about rental laws and mentioned that there should be someone on the team who is familiar with local ordinances. Going hand in hand with keeping the rental in top form is the need to abide by all local ordinances. Tenants who want to get out of paying rent will look for ordinance violations and call the city or county to report a problem as a rent avoidance technique. Once the violation is proven to be true, the investor will be asked to correct it and most likely end up with a fine. Such authority-required repairs cost more since there are deadlines that must be met. The handyman or contractor on the team may be fully booked for weeks with no time to take care of the urgent repairs.

For repairs that affect the tenant's health or well-being, the tenant can legally withhold paying rent. In some states such as California, the tenant can withhold paying rent until the repairs are completed. Also, the tenant could decide to schedule the repairs without the landlord's input and hire an expensive repair person.

In addition to laws applicable to a specific locality, there are Federal and State laws that address things like discrimination based on race, national origin, age, marital status, sexual orientation, and HIV/Aids status. Neglecting those laws can be very costly. The best returns on an investment are returns earned by avoiding costly mistakes.

Some states, cities, and counties have rent control laws that specify how much you can raise your rent or laws that restrict implementing certain fees or charges. Laws commonly found in cities and counties include:

- Laws affecting new locks on rentals.
- Laws affecting R.U.B.S. (Ratio Utility Billing System).
- Rent deposit escrow laws.
- Short-term rental laws.
- Landlord-tenant laws.
- Limit on number of people occupying a rental unit.
- Keeping animals on the premises.
- Operating a business in the house.
- Parking vehicles on or in front of the rental.
- Eviction laws.
- Homeowners Association requirements and limitations.

Each of those laws influences the ability to find tenants, and they may affect the amount of rent collected. Before buying the property, be aware of the impact the laws will have on the asset's operation. If there are uncertainties as to what laws exist in the area, consult with a property manager familiar with the locality.

California, New Jersey, New York, Minnesota, and the District of Columbia allow local jurisdictions to have rent control laws that apply only to those jurisdictions. The Oregon State rent control law applies statewide, and California has a statewide law that limits how much rent can be raised every year. In 2022, several local jurisdictions, especially in California, were considering passing specific rent control laws following skyrocketing rents during the COVID-19 pandemic between 2019 and 2021.

If a property is bought with the intention of constructing an addition, the investor should check with the local jurisdiction regarding the regulations governing such additions. Counties and cities have restrictions on how many units can be built on a lot, how much a built structure can cover the property, how far the addition must be from your neighbor's property, the height of the building, and how you can access and park on the property.

The same is true if a property is bought with the intention of subdividing it and building new rental units. As I stated earlier, there are regulations specifying the minimum lot width, depth, and area. The regulations also specify what type of access must be provided to the newly created lot. If the lot does not meet minimum development requirements, it can't be subdivided and will not be put to the anticipated use. Due diligence is important before committing money to a property.

## Prepare For Real Estate Downturns

Downturns in the overall economy quickly affect the rental market in real estate, and being able to ride out downturns is crucial to any successful investor. Real estate goes through cycles whereby values rise and then fall because of economic conditions. Conversely, downturns in the real estate sector could cause a recession in the overall economy.

Downward cycles are inevitable and are part of a healthy real estate sector. The most recent severe downturn that badly affected real estate was the 2008 housing crash that sent prices all over the country into a nosedive. Investors should prepare for a downturn of some sort, although crashes like the one in 2008 are rare. In the early 1990s, there was an economic downturn in Southern California that was partly caused by military base closures, which led to job losses and a drop in demand for homes. Home prices fell, and lenders repossessed many properties. As an investor, you need to prepare by having cash available to take you through recessions such as those.

I have suggested that for every rental home, there should be at least six months of cash reserves. In economic downturns, people lose jobs and can't pay rent, and therefore, the vacancy rates rise. To avoid a cash shortfall or, even worse, foreclosure, cash reserves are crucial. I have also mentioned that the reserves can be in the form of cash in the bank, a home equity line of credit, in an individual retirement account invested in stocks that you can quickly liquidate. Avoid overleveraging when buying properties and only increase the number of properties as the available reserves grow over time.

Financing homes with adjustable mortgages can worsen the situation in a downturn if the payment adjusts higher. If an adjustable mortgage is used to finance a rental, the interest rate should not adjust in the first ten years. During that time, the loan can be paid down to build equity. The home can then be refinanced or sold for a profit. On estimate, if a property is held for ten years and assuming the typical 7% annual appreciation rate holds, it is highly likely that it can be sold for a decent profit. Downturns in the rental or housing market are something you cannot control, but you can prepare to overcome any negative aspects that arise.

Preparing for economic downturns starts when you pick an area to invest in and acquire the property. Areas with a strong job base, a growing population, and good incomes tend to weather downturns much better than those with a weak job base and a declining population. The size of the population in the area also matters. The bigger the population, the broader the base from which to draw tenants.

It is prudent to have properties that are in demand for different income levels. There are times when one sector of the economy gets hit hardest during the downturn, and many more people working in that sector lose their jobs and can't raise money for rent. So, when picking areas and buying properties, diversify to spread the risk. Economic downturns affect asset classes differently.

A good strategy for successful investing is buying assets in class C areas or better and staying away from class D assets and areas. There is a debate as to whether it is better to buy class C instead of class A assets. It is argued that class C assets fare better in an economic downturn than class A assets. The argument is that class A tenants will move down into class B or class C during a recession, thereby leaving the class A rentals vacant. The counterargument is that class C tenants will move into class A rentals because they become cheaper due to decreases in rent and move-in incentives offered. In addition, the argument goes that in a downturn, it is the white-collar jobs held by class A tenants that are lost. Class C tenants' jobs, which are blue-collar, don't get cut because they are usually essential jobs. Therefore, there are always tenants for the class C properties. No matter what side of the argument you are on, always have a mix of class assets to protect your investment portfolio.

To further protect yourself from the disastrous impacts of downturns, ensure that you buy properties that you can afford to handle. In addition to adequate reserves, having multiple sources of income allows you to weather any loss of income due to vacancies. Keep an eye on the expenses, making sure that you reduce them so as to build up reserves. When appropriate, refinance the loans to reduce mortgage payments. Investors in the game for a long time will, at some point, go through a recession. Going through one affords an experience that you can learn from.

# Chapter 28

# Financing a Property Purchase vs Paying Cash

Occasionally, you will find an investor trying to decide whether to pay cash or to get a loan to buy an investment property. Most investors get loans to buy rental units and take advantage of leverage. The percentage of people who pay cash outright to buy is small. After all, real estate investing is dependent on leverage as a tool to build wealth. The few investors who can pay cash for rental properties wrestle with the question of whether to pay cash or get a loan.

The decision on whether to pay cash or get a loan depends on one's investing strategy. There are advantages and disadvantages to the all-cash approach. Personally, I have borrowed to buy my properties even when I could have paid cash.

## Advantages Of Paying Cash For An Investment Property

1. Personal information is protected: Paying cash eliminates the complexities associated with loan applications, like compiling documents to support the application. Loan approval requires a ton of personal financial documents that are quite intrusive into one's personal life. The lender will know how and where you spend your money and the source and amount of the income. The taxes filed over the

years are submitted with no assurance that the borrower's privacy will be totally protected.

2. Closing on a purchase is fast: With a cash purchase, it takes fewer days to complete the purchase and close on the property. There is no securing of a loan contingency, so the seller will not be kept wondering if the buyer will be approved for the loan.
3. Closing costs are not high: There are no fees that are associated with a loan, such as origination fees, loan broker fees, and private mortgage insurance.
4. Cash buyers get more breaks from the sellers. Sellers prefer buyers who pay cash, and those buyers tend to get more incentives and discounts from the sellers. The sellers want a quick closing and may accept a lower sale price.
5. With a cash purchase, the investor keeps most of the rent collected: Since there is no mortgage to be paid, much of the rental income collected will be pure positive cash flow. Once the property taxes, HOA dues, insurance, and any necessary repairs are paid, the landlord keeps the remaining rental income.
6. No risk of foreclosure: There is no loan on the property, and thus, there is no lender to foreclose on the property. That is one risk that the investor does not have to worry about.

7. Paying cash gives the owner an opportunity for a home equity line of credit (HELOC): With 100% of the equity belonging to the owner, there is always a chance to use the property as collateral to borrow money should there be a need to raise capital.

## Disadvantages Of Paying Cash To Buy Rental Property

1. Capital is tied up in one property: With a cash purchase, the money is tied up since real estate is illiquid. The cash is not available for immediate use since it takes weeks to process a HELOC loan if you need to raise money.
2. Paying cash restricts the ability to scale your business: Assume that you have fifty thousand dollars to invest in real estate and you pay cash for one property, then you can't buy other property using those fifty thousand dollars. However, if you get a loan to buy the home, you will have money left over to acquire additional properties. If you are buying in an area where homes are selling for ten thousand dollars, for example, you could buy four rental homes using those fifty thousand dollars by, say, putting a twenty percent down payment on each of them. There would be money left over for closing costs.
3. The rate of return on investment (ROI) is less when with an all-cash purchase: The rate of return on an investment,

which is expressed as a percentage, measures the profitability of the investment. If an individual invested one hundred dollars to buy an item, turned around, and sold it for one hundred and ten dollars, there is a ten-dollar profit. The rate of return is 10 percent. It is calculated by dividing your $10 profit by the $100 investment and multiplying it by one hundred.

If we take fifty thousand dollars you have for investing and pay cash for one rental house, if the value of that house goes up by one thousand in one year, then the rate of return on your investment ($50,000) is two percent. We took the $1,000 appreciation and divided it by the $50,000 cash invested and came up with 2%.

On the other hand, if you choose to get a loan and put down ten thousand as a down payment, that is the money you have invested. For the sake of simplicity, we will assume that no other expenditures were incurred in the purchase. If, within one year, that property goes up in value for the same one thousand dollars, your rate of return is ten percent. That is much higher and is a preferred rate of return on investment. You calculate the ROI by dividing the $1,000 by the $10,000 invested as a down payment. The person who puts down $10,000 has a better ROI, so he has his money working harder for him.

4. With a cash purchase, the investor misses out on the interest deduction and tax savings: One of the benefits of investing in rental units is being able to deduct the interest

paid on the loan to reduce taxes. That improves the cash flow. Paying cash reduces the cash flow each year.

5. There is less scrutiny and thus higher risks if you pay cash: Less scrutiny increases the chances that mistakes will not be caught. When you apply for a loan, the lender will scrutinize the property to ensure that it meets the standards to get a loan. Lenders will be hesitant to lend money on a property if it has insolvable problems. Also, with cash purchases, the investor is likely not to think of creative ways to save money on the deal.
6. With cash purchase, you increase your chances of being sued: When there is so much equity in a property, there will be someone wanting to come up with a complaint to file a lawsuit. People will be discouraged if they think they can't collect money even when they win a frivolous lawsuit.
7. Having a loan on a property reduces the possibility of title forgeries: We have heard of stories whereby a dishonest individual forges signatures to acquire title to property or take out loans using the property as collateral. This is easier done on properties with no mortgages. The presence of a mortgage requires many additional steps before the title can change hands. Banks, insurance companies, and title companies will be involved. That discourages would-be title thieves.

Paying cash for property or getting a loan depends purely on an investor's circumstances and strategy. To most investors, leveraging their money makes more sense and enables them to scale their business by acquiring more properties. They also enjoy the tax benefits of holding a mortgage. It is up to you as an investor to assess your investment goals and financial situation.

After years of holding on to my rental properties, I came to a point where it was possible to raise money and buy another property without taking out a loan. But was that a good thing for me to do? My strategy is to build wealth in real estate through leveraging, using borrowed money, and watching the value of the properties appreciate as I pay down the loans using tenants' rent.

Discussion of the advantages and disadvantages of paying cash or getting a loan is closely tied to the debate of good versus bad debt. When is it financially appropriate to acquire debt?

## Good Debt

There is plenty written about whether it is a good idea to have debt or not. Is having debt a good thing for an investor, or does debt negatively affect the investor? I have always borrowed money to invest and pursue my real estate goals. As a result, I firmly believe that not all debt is the same. The way I characterize debt depends on what I do with the money I borrow, what I buy, and for what reason. To that effect, some of the debt I have taken on has been good debt, while some others have been bad debt.

Good debt is money I have borrowed to grow my wealth or acquire necessary information and education that allowed me to grow my investments. I consider the debt I took on to acquire real estate as good debt. It is the type of debt that has increased my net worth over time.

This type of debt made me money even when I was not present at the location where the money was invested. I financed the homes with mortgages, rented them out, and used the rent I collected every month to pay down the mortgage. Every month, the loan was paid down, and my net worth grew even when I was many miles away. It allowed me to reduce my tax burden by taking the allowable deductions. I used the money to improve my education and acquire new skills that enabled me to make better-informed decisions. With the debt I took on, I bought things that appreciated in value with time.

Good debt enables you to make money while you sleep. To paraphrase Warren Buffet, if you are not making money while you are sleeping, you will never build wealth, and you will die working for other people.

## Bad Debt

Bad debt is money borrowed to buy things that don't appreciate over time and will instead reduce your net worth as time goes by. Such items include fancy cars or vehicles that do not bring economic value to the work you do. Buying expensive clothes using credit cards, paying for vacations, and dining out at expensive restaurants are also considered bad debts. If not paid off in time, those kinds of debt will result in an accumulation of interest and a decrease in your net worth.

Investors who believe in paying cash for rental units will argue that all debt is bad, including loans taken out for real estate investing. I disagree with the characterization of mortgage debt as bad debt. As shown above, in a discussion about whether to pay cash or get a loan, there are many advantages to financing real estate. The return on investment is a lot higher with financed purchases. Paying cash ties your money down in the property, and it limits the ability to acquire more properties, in addition to eliminating tax savings.

## Raising Money For Starting In Real Estate: My Experiences

It is now evident that money is a necessary ingredient in real estate investing, so the question is how to raise money to start investing. There are several ways to raise money to invest, and I have encountered investors who have devised creative ways to raise the necessary funds.

In the earlier chapters, I touched upon how I came up with money to buy my first primary home and the subsequent properties I acquired. Before I began investing, I was renting an apartment. I had children, and space was a precious commodity in the unit. Children needed room to play and run around. I was focused on buying a house with more space. I had a job, but most of my paycheck went toward rent, buying groceries, and taking care of the children. The challenge was how to save for a down payment and closing costs.

To start, I used a forced saving strategy whereby higher taxes were withheld from my paycheck every two weeks. At the end of the year, there was more money paid toward taxes than was needed. When I filed my taxes, that money was refunded to me, and I put it in a savings account for a down payment. Had that money been available in my paycheck every two weeks, I would have spent it. That turned out to be an excellent way to raise a downpayment. I did not mind that I was giving the government an interest-free loan; the results I got justified my approach.

I took steps to lower my monthly expenses by shopping at discount stores, looking for items on sale, and buying in bulk from big box stores like Sam's Club and Costco. With a big family like I had, it made sense to buy items in bulk, for we always run through them very quickly. It made the price of each item cheaper than if I had bought them in smaller quantities.

Taking care of the children's needs was a huge expense of the family budget, and I was not getting help from their mother. The discount stores sold nice items that were discounted for one reason or another. Trendy stores would discount items because there was a minor manufacturing defect, even though it would not be readily noticeable to an untrained eye. Those items were considered rejects and discounted. I became very well acquainted with where such stores were located. I knew that mall outlets like the one located in Cabazon in Riverside County, California, always had items that were brought in from stores located in expensive areas of Los Angeles and Beverly Hills.

I saved enough money to put down for my first residence, and in 1991, I seriously started looking for homes to buy; I was a willing, able, and ready buyer by that time. In prior years, I would go out to look at homes for sale, but I had no means of buying. During that period when I was saving, I put off buying expensive, big-ticket household items for the apartment. I drove a small, cheap car in which the family barely fit. I was determined to save every penny I could save to buy a home.

That first home I bought by scraping together money ended up being the house that enabled me to buy a second primary residence and, subsequently, several rental homes. I always look at that first house as the seed that I planted and from which other fruit trees grew. Taking money out of properties I already owned that had sufficient equity worked well as a source of investment capital.

Family members are another source of capital needed to start investing. The bank of mom-and-pop, where children borrow money from their parents, has for a long time been known to provide the initial capital for young investors. The pool can be widened to include other relatives beyond mom and dad.

Individuals with money invested in individual retirement accounts can invest it in rental properties. They need to familiarize themselves with the strict Internal Revenue Service regulations governing how the money can be invested. Violations of the regulations can result in huge penalties and a big tax bill; therefore, consult a professional.

The earlier discussed syndications and joint ventures have been used successfully to raise money to buy investment properties. Individuals pool their capital and buy real estate.

Seller financing can also be used to start owning investment properties. This approach works if the property you want to acquire has much equity. Under such arrangements, the seller agrees to act as a lender, offering the buyer a chance to avoid dealing with strict bank lending requirements. If the buyer must get a bank loan, that loan could be small if the seller agrees to finance the purchase.

## Debt Management

Once the investment property is acquired, the work begins to ensure that you don't lose it due to subsequent bad decisions. Managing debt is as important as the decisions you make in choosing an investment area, getting financing, finding good tenants, and building a team. First is the assessment of one's financial situation to avoid taking on debt that one can't afford to pay back. So, know the debts you have and the terms for paying them back, especially the details on the interest rate on the debt and if there is a balloon payment.

Always have a debt payment strategy that shows how the repayments will be handled. Explore plans that result in a shorter repayment period. Above, I talked about snowball and avalanche repayment strategies. Explore additional ways that can enable you to repay the debt and that don't cause extreme stress on the investment portfolio.

Another approach to managing debt is through minimizing expenses and streamlining operations. The money saved can be used to pay down debt by paying more than the minimum payment required each month.

Constantly look for ways to lower debt payments. A seasoned investor will constantly look out for better interest rates to refinance the debt and lower the monthly payments. Don't be afraid to negotiate for better interest rates and loan terms. Every now and then, review the loans to find out where changes can be made. Evaluate the overall debt management strategy occasionally to ensure that it is serving its purpose.

# Chapter 29

## Exit Strategies

Through real estate education and based on my experience, I have concluded that when you decide to buy real estate, especially real estate meant to be held as an investment, one of the most important decisions to make is the exit strategy. Buying investment properties without knowing when and how to sell for a profit is equivalent to walking blindfolded and with absolutely no guidance. In the many training classes and seminars that I attended, there was always an emphasis on having several exit strategies to ensure a profit is made when the asset is sold.

There are several exit strategies that can be used when you decide to invest in real estate, and each has tax advantages and disadvantages. I would not recommend that anyone implement any of the strategies without first consulting a tax professional. Good exit strategies can help you avoid paying high taxes.

If you invest in real estate and sell the property in less than twelve months, then your profits are taxed at the same rate as your ordinary income, which ranges between 10% and 39.6%, depending on your tax bracket. On the other hand, if you own the investment property for over 12 months, those capital gains are taxed at a lower rate. Depending on your taxable income bracket, that rate can be zero, 15%, or 20%. Most investors pay a 15% tax on their long-term capital gains. The taxable income amounts are adjusted yearly. In 2022, IRS long-term capital gain tax rates were as follows:

- Zero taxes for single filers with taxable income of up to $41,675, up to $83,350 for a married couple filing a joint tax return, and for an individual filing as a head of household earning up to $55,800.
- 15% tax rate for single filers with taxable income of up to $459,750, a married couple earning $517,200, up to $258,600 for a married couple filing a separate return, and up to $488,500 for individuals filing as head of household.
- 20% tax rate for single filers with taxable income over $459,750, married couples with taxable income over $517,200, married couples filing a separate return with taxable income of over $258,600, and head of household with income of over $488,500.

**2024 IRS Long-Term Capital Gains Tax Rates**

| Filing Status | No Taxes with taxable income of | 15% tax rate with taxable income of | 20% tax rate with taxable income of |
|---|---|---|---|
| **Single** | Less than $47,025 | $47,026 to $518,900 | Over $518,900 |
| **Married filing a separate return** | Less than $47,025 | $47,026 to $291,850 | Over $291,850 |
| **Head of household** | Less than $63,000 | $63,001 to $551,350 | Over $551,350 |
| **Married filing a joint return** | Less than $94,050 | $94,051 to $583,750 | Over $583,750 |

Source: Internal Revenue Service

As you can see, holding an investment asset for over a year can save you money on taxes.

Investors who convert their primary residence into a rental property can save on taxes if they sell the property within five years of conversion using IRS Section 121. As the name indicates, it is derived from the Internal Revenue Service tax code section 121. That tax code section allows investors to pay no taxes on the profits from selling a home if they have lived in the house for at least two years out of the five years they have held the property.

Under IRS section 121, owners can shelter their profits up to $500,000 for married couples filing a joint return. The amount is half for individual filers or separated couples filing taxes separately. This is a strategy that some tax-savvy individuals use if they know they won't own the property for many years but don't want to sell immediately due to bad market conditions. They can hold on to the property as a rental until the market turns around. Taxes are a major consideration when setting an exit strategy.

Likewise, an investor who owns a rental house can move into that rental and use it as a primary residence for two years. If the investor sells the home after two years, there will be tax savings utilizing IRS Section 121 Exclusion. The investor will have to pay depreciation recapture tax. It is essential to consult a tax professional when using this strategy.

A cash-out exit strategy involves an investor pulling money out of the property. This strategy complements the one discussed above regarding raising money. The money pulled out of the property can be used to acquire more investments in other areas to scale your investments. I am the type of investor who loves to buy and hold to build equity. I have used the cash-out strategy to buy properties successfully.

Another exit strategy commonly used is the "charitable remainder trust (CRT)". This strategy involves donating the rental property to a charitable organization and paying no taxes. The donor becomes the beneficiary and gets an income stream.

As a donor to the charity organization, the IRS allows you to take a deduction on your income, which the IRS code refers to as the net present value of a donation. So, if you are in a position to donate property to a good cause instead of selling and paying taxes on the proceeds, you can consider the charitable remainder trust strategy. Before donating the property, it is advisable to talk to a tax professional who knows the tax code and how the code applies to such donations. Taxes on the transfer could be deferred to a later date. Navigating the donation process can be like walking through a minefield, so take extra precautions to avoid IRS audits and penalties.

An installment sale can also be used as an exit strategy. With an installment sale, the seller collects at least one payment in a tax year and agrees to receive the remaining payments in yearly installments. Typically, the seller retains a security interest in the property until the buyer makes the final payment. The advantage of using an installment sale agreement, among other things, is that you pay taxes at a lower rate. Taxes are collected only on the principal paid that particular year. If you are having a hard time finding a buyer, using an installment sale can help speed up the sale of your property. There are many other advantages of this type of exit strategy, but as with other strategies, plan and use a professional.

Internal Revenue Section 72 allows the transfer of property into a private annuity trust (PAT). Under this strategy, you, as the owner, become the annuitant giving the rental property to a trust. While the trust owns the property, it can pay you regular payments that can last for as long as you are alive. During the transfer, the capital gains taxes and depreciation recapture are deferred. As advised before, I recommend you get a professional to assist you.

A common strategy used by real estate investors is the 1031 like-kind exchange, which is named after the Internal Revenue Service tax code section 1031. The exchange allows the sale of a rental property and defer paying taxes if you can buy a property like the one you just sold. It requires identifying the like-kind property within 45 days of the sale. The entire process must be completed no later than 180 days. The IRS requires such exchanges to be accomplished through a qualified intermediary.

The emphasis in this strategy is on like-kind property. The properties involved in the exchange must be held for investment or business purposes. According to the IRS, properties involved in the exchange "…are of like-kind if they're of the same nature or character, even if they differ in grade or quality." (source IRS Publication 544 – Sales and Other Dispositions of Assets) Also, the investor must take on as much or greater debt with the acquisition. The proceeds from the sale cannot be used for anything else other than buying a like-kind property.

Escrow for such exchanges should be handled by someone knowledgeable of the IRS rules because a slight mix-up could result in a hefty capital gains tax bill. Two of the rules most neglected are:

- Failure to identify the maximum of 3 properties as the replacement properties.
- The 200% rule which restricts the maximum value of the identified properties to no more than 200% of the property that is sold.

Another way to exit an investment and manage capital gains taxes is to sell the property through seller financing, where you act as the lender by holding a promissory note on the property. As the seller, you retain a lien or deed of trust on the property as collateral until the loan is paid in full. The title transfers to the buyer at closing, but you receive payments in installments over time rather than a lump sum. Using the installment sale method under IRS rules, you can defer capital gains taxes by reporting the gain proportionately as you receive payments on the principal. This approach spreads the tax liability over multiple years, potentially lowering your annual tax burden and keeping you in a lower tax bracket.

This strategy can be reversed and used to acquire property if you, as an investor, identify a seller willing to finance your purchase. I touched upon this strategy above as one of the ways to buy property.

Just like choosing the best strategy to start investing in real estate, the exit strategy is a personal decision, and not one strategy fits every investor. The decision should be based on one's circumstances, the economic conditions in the area, and the health of the real estate market.

On my part, I evaluated the investment options that were available to me. Investing close to home had proven to be advantageous given my initial limited experience in being a landlord at the time. After four years, I bought out-of-state properties. I took money out of one rental house to buy others. My intention was to buy cash-flowing properties, hold on to them, and exit when they had appreciated in value. The goal was to trade up to more expensive properties using a 1031 Exchange.

When I started investing in apartments as a partner, the exit strategies implemented turned out to be very different. For one, I started as a limited partner, which meant that I had limited say in how the exit strategies were set. As a member of the syndication team, I was presented with investment deals that were found by other individuals who acted as general partners. They put up a big chunk of the purchase money and made the important decisions. I invested in the property if I found their exit strategy acceptable. Typical exit strategies in apartment investing involve setting an initial hold period of five to seven years. After that initial period, the property is either sold or the loan refinanced and investors who wish to get their money back do so while sharing in the equity gained over the hold period.

# Chapter 30

# Enjoy and Celebrate the Results of Your Hard Work

You have worked hard to start investing; you looked for capital, researched areas to invest in, and found properties to buy. You interviewed property managers, found tenants, and dealt with their demands. You have probably sold some of your assets and realized a profit. It is time to celebrate your work and achievements. Celebrate your accomplishments with friends and family because successful real estate investing is not an easy thing to do. Many people start out trying to acquire investment property, but only a few of them end up successful. It takes a lot of work and perseverance to be a successful investor.

As you celebrate, it is a good time to bring together people you collaborated with, especially if you formed a partnership to buy the property. Celebrating has the advantage of keeping you motivated on your journey to build your real estate portfolio and building your confidence. It offers an opportunity to inform others of what you do and a chance to recruit investors you can collaborate with on future deals.

## Relations With Your Friends After Real Estate

When you succeed in your real estate ventures, you may find that you have to form new friendships that will help you solve issues that come up and discuss your ideas. These are the people who understand what you do. They are people with whom you have things in common regarding investing. The worst thing in real estate investing is to take advice from people with little or no knowledge of what you do. You will run into people who will claim to know a lot and are very willing to advise you. When you encounter such people, you need to remember that little knowledge can turn out to be very dangerous. You don't want to lose your investment because you took bad advice.

After I bought several investment properties, I found out that many of my friends were not the group of people I could call to talk about issues that I came across in my investment activities. Real estate investing involves acquiring specialized knowledge through training and practice.

Forming circles of fellow investors to talk about your ventures makes investment discussions less awkward. To non-real estate investors, talking about issues you encounter investing comes across as bragging. People will start to resent being around you if that is all you talk about. There were occasions when people just walked away or made negative comments whenever I talked about my investments. One person told me that I did not belong to the group of friends any longer.

When you find yourself in that kind of environment, you realize that whatever you talk about, even when it is not real estate-related, there is little connection. A discussion that involves investing does not unite you in any way. You start to notice that you have completely different goals, and your views on financial matters are far apart.

As investors, we must recruit new people to work with as we celebrate our achievements. It is a good idea to be tactful when talking about what you do so as not to alienate future investors who are vital to your success. The key is to identify individuals who realize the value of investing. Follow up with them in a non-group setting and offer them more information about real estate investing. There will be people who realize that keeping company with someone who knows more about what they are interested in is beneficial.

## Stay Informed Of Changes In Real Estate

It is not uncommon for people to over-celebrate to the point where they ignore their duties. People who have realized success can get set in their ways and forget or ignore changes happening in the industry. There are individuals who get firmly tied to the past and end up lagging behind new ideas and inventions. It is important to keep being innovative and not be content with what you have gotten. Adapt to changes that may happen over time. It may be human nature to resist change; however, doing so could lead to an investment downfall. I have seen people who got stuck in the past, where the past was always prominently featured, and who resisted new ideas and changes. That is a recipe for realizing minimal results or even failure.

Similarly, being stuck in negativity deprives one of the ability to come up with new ideas that help to improve one's well-being. If someone spends all their time trying to come up with something negative to say about someone, that individual is not thinking about finding another investment opportunity.

In addition, negativity affects an individual's emotional state, which also affects their creative ability.

## Be Aware Of The Reasons Why People Fail To Invest In Real Estate

It is true that many people, especially minorities, avoid investing in real estate. When I started investing in real estate in the early 2000s, I would walk into a room full of investors, and I would be the only member of a minority group in the room. There are several reasons why we tend to avoid real estate investing:

- Homeownership is not common, especially in minority-dominated neighborhoods. Many people cannot afford to buy homes in those areas. Incomes tend to be low to afford to buy a home. Therefore, people tend to be renters.
- Individuals are not familiar with how to use leverage to acquire property. Successful real estate investors know the value of borrowed money and have acquired skills in using debt to grow their wealth. They are able to put down a fraction of the purchase price and acquire debt to finance the purchase.
- The formal educational systems rarely teach financial literacy. Most people learn about real estate investment strategies from the people they associate with on a regular basis in an informal setting. Individuals will not invest in real estate if they are surrounded and influenced by people who don't see real estate as a vehicle for building wealth.

## Adapt To Changes In The Real Estate Market And The Area In Which You Invest

While working at the City of Riverside, there was a time when my department went through a major reorganization, and almost everyone in the department found themselves having to deal with changes. Like many employees, I found myself having a hard time dealing with changes and adapting to the new work environment. One of the employees recommended that I get hold of and read a book titled "Who Moved My Cheese? by Dr. Spencer Johnson. She recommended this book, saying that it addressed many of the issues and situations happening in the department with the reorganization and that the book would help me succeed in the workplace.

The book, which references two mice and two humans, examines how they behave when they find themselves in a maze. It stresses that we need to realize the new normal, and the quicker we do so and get away from the past, the better we can be. The sooner you let go of the old cheese, the faster you will find new cheese.

I found the book relevant to people I have encountered in my life, both in the USA and in other countries. Some people stick to old customs for too long, failing to work on things that help them pull themselves up and start building wealth.

Some of us are used to seeing successful people or powerful individuals in our old societies going to work wearing a necktie and a suit. Those now outdated images of what success and status are supposed to look like make us pass on opportunities that cross our paths in life. We refuse to take on jobs where we will not wear a suit, and we spend time looking for suit and necktie jobs and, in many instances, without success. So, our lives are spent in that frame of mind. Now, if you had strategically taken on a job that helped you achieve your investment goal, even though it did not require wearing a suit, you could have been able to build wealth. Such a job could enable you to raise a down payment or qualify for a loan and act as a necessary bridge to your investment goals. Getting stuck in the old ways can result in losses.

Know yourself and be comfortable with who you are. There are a lot of negativities that will come your way, and if you don't know yourself, your aspirations will not be realized. I have been attacked with negative talk and given so many negative labels. My ability to withstand all the negative attacks that I have experienced is because I strongly believed in myself and what I could accomplish. Had I failed to hold on to my beliefs and convictions and known that I was not the terrible person that I was being labeled, I would not have been able to put my children through school on a single income and build my investment portfolio. Know how to deal with negativity and use that energy as inspiration to pursue your goals.

Those individuals who come after you with put-downs and negativity are the people you should use as a driving force to reach for what you may have originally thought impossible.

When raising my children, I prayed that they grow up and not make judgments of people based on anything other than their achievements in life. I hoped that I portrayed an example of that by not judging people by looking at where they are from but by looking at what they have done and achieved in their time on this planet earth. I came to realize that the root cause of social injustices we encounter in our lives is rooted in the concept of looking at people from afar and judging them solely on their external appearance without getting to know them.

To be successful, you must be a sponge, absorbing much of the information that comes your way. At the same time, you must be an effective filter, able to determine what information is true and useful and which information is false to deserve ignoring.

For people of color, it is common to be labeled crazy and or not knowing what you are doing. We may be in the twenty-first century, but the white savior attitudes in society are still with us. There will be people who see you investing in real estate and feel an obligation to save you from yourself, believing that you are on a path of self-destruction. They believe that they must come and save you from yourself. It has happened to me on several occasions. If you haven't done your research and have not educated yourself, this might discourage you and start to doubt yourself. Don't be discouraged, and don't give up.

Based on the lessons I have learned, building wealth through real estate investing may sound like an impossible endeavor; however, it is achievable. The best time to start investing is now. Start by setting up a strategy and developing an investment plan. Once you set investment goals, implement them gradually, one at a time. Take time to learn, soak up as much information as you can, and embrace new technologies and ideas introduced in real estate. Never stop learning. Associate yourself with people who will help you grow and enhance your investing skills and avoid negative people who are there to discourage you and pull you down. Pick areas to invest carefully, avoiding bad locations and bad properties. Focus on properties with positive cash flow. Always use the tax breaks the tax code allows you. I learned many lessons from stories told by investors, and I hope my story and experiences help at least one person achieve their wealth-building goals.

Always take action to help someone's life take a different and better direction. Experiencing a sense of accomplishment after helping someone in need is profoundly rewarding. It's more than just lending a hand; it's about being part of a transformative journey. Witnessing someone's life take a different, better direction because of your support fills you with a deep sense of purpose and fulfillment. It's knowing that your actions contributed to a positive change in another person's life, whether big or small. Ultimately, this sense of accomplishment is a reminder that we all have the potential to make a lasting impact on others' lives. Some of those individuals may show no appreciation, but you will have a sense of accomplishment.

www.ingramcontent.com/pod-product-compliance
Lightning Source LLC
LaVergne TN
LVHW052248200926
848481LV00002B/305
* 9 7 9 8 3 4 9 3 4 0 6 3 5 *